The Yosemite

THE JOHN MUIR LIBRARY

The Mountains of California
The Story of My Boyhood and Youth
Travels in Alaska
The Yosemite

JOHN MUIR

The Yosemite

SIERRA CLUB BOOKS · SAN FRANCISCO

Foreword Copyright © 1988 by David Brower

Library of Congress Cataloging-in-Publication Data

Muir, John, 1838–1914.
    The Yosemite.

    Reprint. Originally published: Boston: Houghton Mifflin, 1914.
    Includes index.
        1. Yosemite National Park (Calif.)   2. Yosemite Valley (Calif.)
I. Title.
F868.Y6M9   1988   979.4'47   87-23573
ISBN 0-87156-782-2 (pbk.)

Book design and illustrations by Michael McCurdy
Production by Susan Ristow
Composition by Wilsted & Taylor Publishing Services

Printed in the United States of America on acid-free paper containing a minimum of 50% recovered waste paper, of which at least 10% of the fiber content is post-consumer waste

10 9 8 7

Affectionately dedicated to my friend,
Robert Underwood Johnson,
faithful lover and defender of our
glorious forests and originator
of the Yosemite National Park.

Contents

Acknowledgment

On the early history of Yosemite the writer is indebted to Prof. J. D. Whitney for quotations from his volume entitled "Yosemite Guide-Book," and to Dr. Bunnell for extracts from his interesting volume entitled "Discovery of the Yosemite."

Foreword

"Climb the mountains
and get their glad tidings . . . "

FROM his first discovery of Yosemite in 1868 until Christmas Eve,
1914, when he died, John Muir believed that Yosemite was one of
the most important places on Earth. Herein you will see what great
joy Yosemite brought him. Indeed, it is quite likely that what San
Francisco was about to do to kill Hetch Hetchy Valley, the second
Yosemite Valley within Yosemite National Park, instilled the huge
grief that hastened his death.

This edition of a book Muir wrote when he was seventy-three
is being published seventy-three years after his death and seventy-
five after the birth of this disciple of his. By coincidence, a Secretary of the Interior, with whom one of us has heartily disagreed,
has taken the steps that ought to lead to Hetch Hetchy's being returned to Yosemite. An earlier Secretary of the Interior, with the
help of Congress, let Hetch Hetchy be destroyed. I would like to
see it restored, and so would the Sierra Club that John Muir
founded. So should the City of San Francisco, which led the disas-
trous invasion of Yosemite and the national park idea.

The national park idea itself was then so new that it was vul-
nerable to attack. It was born in California five years before John
Muir arrived in Yosemite, which was four years before Yellowstone
National Park was established in 1872.

The idea is that a deserving place itself, and the resources
within it, are not for sale. Its natural beauty is to be protected so
that it can always be informing and be enjoyed for itself.

Foreword

For thousands of years, the first Americans were able to do just that. Their technology and their understanding of nature were sophisticated enough to let them live in the wilderness without impairing it.

Those who lived in the valley named after them must surely have known how beautiful a spot it was. They had traveled the Sierra freely, on foot. Sharp eyes are still finding the arrowheads the Indians let fly but could not recover. People are still discovering them in remote parts of the High Sierra.

There are probably many places that provide clear evidence of the early Americans' eye for beauty, but I know of only one. Just above Tully Hole, near where the San Joaquin River's high sloping meadows give way to McGee Creek Pass, just a few miles southeast of Yosemite National Park, there is a magnificent place to stop for a broad view and a long rest as you labor toward the pass.

There, with this fine panorama spread out for all to see, are four well-spaced mounds of obsidian chips. Don't look for arrowheads. All that remains are the bits which, as they were chipped away, were to reveal arrowheads. Thousands of bits accumulated year after year, perhaps century after century, as the earliest Sierra explorers traveled their trade route from the eastern Sierra sources of obsidian. They passed en route to enjoy what they saw, meanwhile making miniature spires of glass in the image of the spires of granite on the Sierra crest.

Perhaps a few thousand years after the Indians had first crossed there, members of the Joseph Walker party of 1833 crossed the Sierra from the east. They followed the divide between Hetch Hetchy's Tuolumne River and Yosemite's Merced. From one of their camps they explored the terrain just south of their route and looked

Foreword

down upon Yosemite Valley. They came out on the rim, presumably just west of the Upper Yosemite Fall, thus missing the Indian Canyon route the earlier explorers used freely, hardly a mile to the east. Perhaps the Walker party had no wish to make the three-thousand-foot descent to the Yosemite Valley floor or to face the three thousand feet they would have to climb back up.

Eighteen years later the Mariposa Battalion, led by Major Lafayette Bunnell, made the first white visit to the valley floor, arriving there in pursuit of the Yosemite Indians. Their invasion was once called the discovery of Yosemite, but the Indians could properly question the claim. The soldiers were not concerned about endangered cultures, being more bent on endangering them. They pursued the Yosemites up to Tenaya Lake, named it after the Yosemites' chief, and extradited the natives to the flatland of the San Joaquin Valley, from Paradise directly to the Ninth Circle.

That was in 1851. Four years later Thomas Ayers, accompanying the first tourist party, arrived to make the first drawing of Yosemite. Four more years brought C. L. Weed, Ansel Adams's first predecessor with a lens. Word got out and the siege was on, small-scale. Not a moment too soon came the man who was to enunciate the national park idea with clarity and force—Frederick Law Olmsted. John Muir has been called the father of the national parks. Olmsted was at least the grandfather.

Mountains, unable to vote or protect themselves, need a voice, and Olmsted was one of the first to try to speak for them. After working several years to establish New York's Central Park, Olmsted resigned in 1863, was named superintendent of the Sierra mining estates of General Fremont in Mariposa, and became deeply interested in Yosemite. He was the right man in the right

Foreword

place at the right time. With Yosemite in mind he proposed the rights for landscape implicit in the national park idea. The first requirement, he said, is to preserve the natural scenery and restrict within the narrowest limits the necessary accommodation of visitors. Structures should not detract from the dignity of the scene. "In permitting the sacrifice of anything that would be of the slightest value to future visitors," he wrote, "to the convenience, bad taste, playfulness, carelessness, or wanton destructiveness of present visitors, we probably yield in each case the interest of uncounted millions to the selfishness of a few."

Thus was an idea conceived by an East-coaster delivered to the West. The world would later contribute to its maturing.

In 1868, John Muir began his own contribution, one that would continue for the ensuing forty-six years. He had just arrived in Oakland. Behind him were Scotland, Wisconsin, an unsympathetic father, assorted inventions, and a thousand-mile walk to the Gulf of Mexico. Oakland found him ready to say to the first person who asked where he wanted to go, "Anywhere that's wild."

John Muir found what he wanted in the Sierra: wildness—something more vital than mere scenery—and the wild creatures and plants and space and sky and light that belonged there. He would also find domestic creatures that did not. He watched them all, and wrote and talked about them. There was a bit more color in his language than would be expected today, but it was expected then, and relished fully.

Writers occasionally move editors, and Muir moved his, and was in turn urged to gather some friends together to save the Sierra from sheep. Muir had seen more sheep than he cared to, as he revealed in his book *My First Summer in the Sierra* (the Sierra

Foreword

Club's version, illustrated by Richard Kauffman, is a must). The man who urged him was Robert Underwood Johnson, editor of *Century Magazine*. He had camped with Muir in Yosemite in 1889. Muir was persuasive; in 1890 Johnson had the bill to establish Yosemite National Park introduced in Congress. And Johnson was persuasive, too. The Sierra Club was founded in 1892, and the club would find more than sheep to save the Sierra from.

Led by Muir and colleagues, principally from the faculties of the University of California and Stanford, augmented by lawyers, the club almost immediately plunged into vigorous legislative activity and has seldom let up since.

OLMSTED had stated the essence of the park idea in 1865, a year after Yosemite Valley and the Mariposa Grove of Big Trees were set aside as a park to be protected for the nation. But it is one thing to call for protection, and another to provide it. Congress delegated to the State of California the task of administration and enforcement. When Yellowstone was set aside by Congress eight years later, there was no State of Wyoming to delegate to; Wyoming remained a territory until 1890. So the United States retained full jurisdiction of Yellowstone National Park, but not of Yosemite.

In 1890, when Congress established the greater Yosemite area as Yosemite National Park, the United States retained jurisdiction over all but Yosemite Valley and the Mariposa Grove. But jurisdiction does not provide protection automatically. From his earliest Sierra days John Muir had seen the importance of building a constituency to protect Yosemite. If people knew about a special place, they would want to protect it.

Muir had managed, by word and sketch, to let them know.

Foreword

He did not write and sketch just for future visitors, but for scientists as well. Some of them did not welcome his ideas. One of these, the eminent geologist Josiah Dwight Whitney, believed that Yosemite Valley had been nothing at all until the bottom dropped out of it, leaving the walls. This would have been no minor cataclysm. But Muir would have none of it. He had walked too much of the country on foot to agree with Whitney's hypothesis. Muir read the evidence of glaciation well. He was forever asking Why? and coming up with his own good answers. Senior geologists do not like this from a thirty-one-year-old kid, but Muir was determined. His keen observations of the habits of glaciers first appeared at length in a series of seven articles in the *Overland Monthly* in 1874 and 1875. The articles were reprinted after his death in the Sierra Club Bulletin from 1915 to 1921, and were gathered together and published in book form by the club in 1950. His observations, then at least seventy-five years old, stood up well and they still do.

I have the bad habit, when not watched, of asking scientists what they most devoutly believe now that is most likely to be laughed at in twenty-five years. The question sobers the scientist.

So here is Muir, more than a century later, still holding up. True, he had overestimated the extent of glaciation and underestimated its frequency (according to present beliefs), but he wiped out Professor Whitney. And if you, too, are inclined to underestimate the power of a glacier, go to the Ahwahnee Meadow. Look up at Glacier Point, thirty-two hundred feet above you. Look west seven miles to El Capitan, where the old moraine is just about on your level. Look back at Half Dome, a mile higher than you are. Now guess how deep the ancient glaciers plowed into the solid granite beneath you, to give old Lake Yosemite its space. Fossil

Foreword

Lake Yosemite still lurks there among all the things the Merced River and Tenaya Creek could carry to fill it up with, but you can't see it.

How deep? In 1930 the eminent geomorphologist Francois Matthes, whose typographic maps are some of the most beautiful you will ever see, thought the lake was two or three hundred feet deep at most, and thought Muir had exaggerated the glacier's power.

In the 1940s, geologist John P. Buwalda did what Matthes was not equipped to do. Professor Buwalda measured the depth scismically.

How deep was old Lake Yosemite?

Half a mile. It would not be a good idea to stand in the way of an advancing, determined glacier.

MUIR was happy enough with what the glaciers were doing for Yosemite, but not with what California's Yosemite commissioners were doing to it. To get people to see the Valley, he wanted more roads and hotels than the commissioners wanted. They were not happy about his working in a sawmill near the foot of Lower Yosemite Fall. They also favored the idea of controlled burning—the periodic setting of fires, Indian-style, to keep the Valley floor more open and also to prevent the excessive accumulation of fuel (young trees, brush, and litter) that could endanger the forest as a whole. Muir disagreed. The commissioners did not think it was wrong for the state to manage Yosemite National Park's most famous gems, the Valley and the Big Tree Grove. Muir did. In the end, Muir, the Sierra Club, and the Southern Pacific Railroad prevailed. The Valley and the Grove were ceded back to the United States.

Foreword

There was as yet no National Park Service to administer and protect Yosemite or any of the other national parks. The U.S. Army filled in. A Yosemite High Sierra lake is named after Colonel Harry C. Benson, the Army's superintendent of Yosemite from 1905 to 1908. The colonel must have pleased Muir with his handling of sheepherders who let their flocks invade northern Yosemite. The sheepherders were arrested and transported to the far side of the national park, the sheep meanwhile were driven out and freed.

The invasion of the sheepherders was a minor one compared to San Francisco's. The city claimed that it must secure its water supply by damming Hetch Hetchy Valley. No other way would do. It alleged that the reservoir would be more beautiful than the virgin valley and that the dam would be easily covered with grasses and vines. What the city really wanted was the difference in elevation between Hetch Hetchy Valley, at 3800 feet, and Mocassin Creek powerhouse, at 800 feet. If the city could control the flow of the Tuolumne River over the course of that drop, a substantial amount of profitable hydroelectric energy could be generated.

Muir, the Sierra Club, and many other organizations fought hard, but lost, and a second Yosemite Valley was denied the public. The story of Muir's battle is best told in *John Muir and the Sierra Club: The Story of Yosemite*, a book that had a limited distribution and ought to be republished in paperback to help America get Hetch Hetchy back.

The Sierra Club leaders were themselves split in the Hetch Hetchy battle, and John Muir and William Colby, his chief lieutenant, had to set up a separate organization to carry on their fight until the matter was finally put to a vote of the members. In this vote Muir and Colby won handily.

Foreword

The war, however, was lost—lost to "practical men," people who, in the words of Disraeli, have made all their decisions, have lost the ability to listen, and are determined to perpetuate the errors of their ancestors. Such people are not yet an endangered species.

Even practical men might well have heeded Olmsted had they read his report, but that document was lost for eighty years, and was not to reappear until the 1950s. In any event, Olmsted was a landscape architect, and not widely read in the new State of California. He was, however, heard by his son, also a landscape architect, Frederick Law Olmsted, *fils*. The son was ready when the Hetch Hetchy disaster riveted attention on the need for an agency that could adequately protect the parks. His father's vision, the son saw to it, was written into the National Park Act of 1916, providing that the natural beauty and wildlife in the national parks were to be used and enjoyed by the public by such means as would leave the landscape unimpaired, this to be enjoyed by the uncounted millions of future visitors.

To use without impairing is not easy. A national park is not quite a museum, where you may look but not touch. In a park you need to drive or walk or climb to look. Cars leave more lasting footprints than people do, so one solution is to walk more—and thus make the park bigger because it takes so much longer to walk through it. Cars are much harder to discipline than are walkers, and highway builders harder still. Climbers are far more amenable to reason than cars are. Modern climbers are embarrassingly less wearing of Yosemite cliffs than my generation of climbers was. They are more inclined to depend upon boldness and genius. So was Muir in his climbs.

But Muir was right in not wanting perfect protection. Glen Canyon, on the Colorado River, was "the place no one knew," and

Foreword

it was flooded. A few people actually knew about it, as a few people knew about Hetch Hetchy. But not enough of them, or enough about it.

As you read about and enjoy what Yosemite meant to John Muir, and as you realize what he meant to Yosemite, and what his interpretation of Yosemite will always mean because it will always be in print somewhere, please do him a favor. Join with people everywhere who appreciate the bold suggestion of Secretary of the Interior Don Hodel. Give the Hetch Hetchy Yosemite back to its original owners—all of us and all our children and theirs and all the natural things that should be living there forever. Require San Francisco to get its water from exactly where it now gets it—from the Tuolumne River just below Mocassin Creek powerhouse. More water will be available there if it is no longer wastefully evaporated from Hetch Hetchy reservoir. The Tuolumne River can be adequately controlled at what was the best place in the first place— the site where Don Pedro reservoir was built, too late. It holds half a dozen times more water than Hetch Hetchy does. Let San Francisco get its electricity from where everybody else does—not from a national park.

If Hetch Hetchy is restored and the world has the opportunity to watch the slow but beautifully inevitable recovery of a once sublime valley, you can smile again, John Muir, wherever you are.

". . . and do something to make the mountains glad."

David Brower
August 1987

The Yosemite

1

The Approach to the Valley

WHEN I set out on the long excursion that finally led to California I wandered afoot and alone, from Indiana to the Gulf of Mexico, with a plant-press on my back, holding a generally southward course, like the birds when they are going from summer to winter. From the west coast of Florida I crossed the gulf to Cuba, enjoyed the rich tropical flora there for a few months, intending to go thence to the north end of South America, make my way through the woods to the headwaters of the Amazon, and float down that grand river to the ocean. But I was unable to find a ship bound for South America—fortunately perhaps, for I had incredibly little money for so long a trip and had not yet fully recovered from a fever caught in the Florida swamps. Therefore I decided to visit California for a year or two to see its wonderful flora and the famous Yosemite Valley. All the world was before me and every day was a holiday, so it did not seem important to which one of the world's wildernesses I first should wander.

Arriving by the Panama steamer, I stopped one day in San Francisco and then inquired for the nearest way out of town. "But where do you want to go?" asked the man to whom I had applied for this important information. "To any place that is wild," I said. This reply startled him. He seemed to fear I might be crazy and therefore the sooner I was out of town the better, so he directed me to the Oakland ferry.

The Yosemite

So on the first of April, 1868, I set out afoot for Yosemite. It was the bloom-time of the year over the lowlands and coast ranges; the landscapes of the Santa Clara Valley were fairly drenched with sunshine, all the air was quivering with the songs of the meadow-larks, and the hills were so covered with flowers that they seemed to be painted. Slow indeed was my progress through these glorious gardens, the first of the California flora I had seen. Cattle and cultivation were making few scars as yet, and I wandered enchanted in long wavering curves, knowing by my pocket map that Yosemite Valley lay to the east and that I should surely find it.

THE SIERRA FROM THE WEST

Looking eastward from the summit of the Pacheco Pass one shining morning, a landscape was displayed that after all my wanderings still appears as the most beautiful I have ever beheld. At my feet lay the Great Central Valley of California, level and flowery, like a lake of pure sunshine, forty or fifty miles wide, five hundred miles long, one rich furred garden of yellow *Compositœ*. And from the eastern boundary of this vast golden flower-bed rose the mighty Sierra, miles in height, and so gloriously colored and so radiant, it seemed not clothed with light, but wholly composed of it, like the wall of some celestial city. Along the top and extending a good way down, was a rich pearl-gray belt of snow; below it a belt of blue and dark purple, marking the extension of the forests; and stretching along the base of the range a broad belt of rose-purple; all these colors, from the blue sky to the yellow valley smoothly blending as they do in a rainbow, making a wall of light ineffably fine. Then it seemed to me that the Sierra should be called, not the Nevada or

The Approach to the Valley

Snowy Range, but the Range of Light. And after ten years of wandering and wondering in the heart of it, rejoicing in its glorious floods of light, the white beams of the morning streaming through the passes, the noonday radiance on the crystal rocks, the flush of the alpenglow, and the irised spray of countless waterfalls, it still seems above all others the Range of Light.

In general views no mark of man is visible upon it, nor anything to suggest the wonderful depth and grandeur of its sculpture. None of its magnificent forest-crowned ridges seems to rise much above the general level to publish its wealth. No great valley or river is seen, or group of well-marked features of any kind standing out as distinct pictures. Even the summit peaks, marshaled in glorious array so high in the sky, seem comparatively regular in form. Nevertheless the whole range five hundred miles long is furrowed with cañons 2000 to 5000 feet deep, in which once flowed majestic glaciers, and in which now flow and sing the bright rejoicing rivers.

CHARACTERISTICS OF THE CAÑONS

Though of such stupendous depth, these cañons are not gloomy gorges, savage and inaccessible. With rough passages here and there they are flowery pathways conducting to the snowy, icy fountains; mountain streets full of life and light, graded and sculptured by the ancient glaciers, and presenting throughout all their courses a rich variety of novel and attractive scenery—the most attractive that has yet been discovered in the mountain ranges of the world. In many places, especially in the middle region of the western flank, the main cañons widen into spacious valleys or parks diversified like landscape gardens with meadows and groves and thickets

[3]

The Yosemite

of blooming bushes, while the lofty walls, infinitely varied in form, are fringed with ferns, flowering plants, shrubs of many species, and tall evergreens and oaks that find footholds on small benches and tables, all enlivened and made glorious with rejoicing streams that come chanting in chorus over the cliffs and through side cañons in falls of every conceivable form, to join the river that flows in tranquil, shining beauty down the middle of each one of them.

THE INCOMPARABLE YOSEMITE

The most famous and accessible of these cañon valleys, and also the one that presents their most striking and sublime features on the grandest scale, is the Yosemite, situated in the basin of the Merced River at an elevation of 4000 feet above the level of the sea. It is about seven miles long, half a mile to a mile wide, and nearly a mile deep in the solid granite flank of the range. The walls are made up of rocks, mountains in size, partly separated from each other by side cañons, and they are so sheer in front, and so compactly and harmoniously arranged on a level floor, that the Valley, comprehensively seen, looks like an immense hall or temple lighted from above.

But no temple made with hands can compare with Yosemite. Every rock in its walls seems to glow with life. Some lean back in majestic repose; others, absolutely sheer or nearly so for thousands of feet, advance beyond their companions in thoughtful attitudes, giving welcome to storms and calms alike, seemingly aware, yet heedless, of everything going on about them. Awful in stern, immovable majesty, how softly these rocks are adorned, and how fine and reassuring the company they keep: their feet among beautiful groves and meadows, their brows in the sky, a thousand flowers leaning confidingly against their feet, bathed in floods of water, floods of light, while the snow and waterfalls, the winds and avalanches and clouds shine and sing and wreathe about them as the years go by, and myriads of small winged creatures—birds, bees, butterflies—give glad animation and help to make all the air into music. Down through the middle of the Valley flows the crystal Merced, River of Mercy, peacefully quiet, reflecting lilies and trees and the onlooking rocks; things frail and fleeting and types of endurance meeting here and blending in countless forms, as if into this one mountain mansion Nature had gathered her choicest treasures, to draw her lovers into close and confiding communion with her.

THE APPROACH TO THE VALLEY

Sauntering up the foothills to Yosemite by any of the old trails or roads in use before the railway was built from the town of Merced up the river to the boundary of Yosemite Park, richer and wilder become the forests and streams. At an elevation of 6000 feet above the level of the sea the silver firs are 200 feet high, with branches whorled around the colossal shafts in regular order, and every branch beautifully pinnate like a fern frond. The Douglas spruce, the yellow and sugar pines and brown-barked Libocedrus here reach their finest developments of beauty and grandeur. The majestic Sequoia is here, too, the king of conifers, the noblest of all the noble race. These colossal trees are as wonderful in fineness of beauty and proportion as in stature—an assemblage of conifers surpassing all that have ever yet been discovered in the forests of

The Yosemite

the world. Here indeed is the tree-lover's paradise; the woods, dry and wholesome, letting in the light in shimmering masses of half sunshine, half shade; the night air as well as the day air indescribably spicy and exhilarating; plushy fir-boughs for campers' beds, and cascades to sing us to sleep. On the highest ridges, over which these old Yosemite ways passed, the silver fir (*Abies magnifica*) forms the bulk of the woods, pressing forward in glorious array to the very brink of the Valley walls on both sides, and beyond the Valley to a height of from 8000 to 9000 feet above the level of the sea. Thus it appears that Yosemite, presenting such stupendous faces of bare granite, is nevertheless imbedded in magnificent forests, and the main species of pine, fir, spruce and libocedrus are also found in the Valley itself, but there are no "big trees" (*Sequoia gigantea*) in the Valley or about the rim of it. The nearest are about ten and twenty miles beyond the lower end of the valley on small tributaries of the Merced and Tuolumne Rivers.

THE FIRST VIEW: THE BRIDAL VEIL

From the margin of these glorious forests the first general view of the Valley used to be gained—a revelation in landscape affairs that enriches one's life forever. Entering the Valley, gazing overwhelmed with the multitude of grand objects about us, perhaps the first to fix our attention will be the Bridal Veil, a beautiful waterfall on our right. Its brow, where it first leaps free from the cliff, is about 900 feet above us; and as it sways and sings in the wind, clad in gauzy, sun-sifted spray, half falling, half floating, it seems infinitely gentle and fine; but the hymns it sings tell the solemn fateful power hidden beneath its soft clothing.

The Approach to the Valley

The Bridal Veil shoots free from the upper edge of the cliff by the velocity the stream has acquired in descending a long slope above the head of the fall. Looking from the top of the rock-avalanche talus on the west side, about one hundred feet above the foot of the fall, the under surface of the water arch is seen to be finely grooved and striated; and the sky is seen through the arch between rock and water, making a novel and beautiful effect.

Under ordinary weather conditions the fall strikes on flat-topped slabs, forming a kind of ledge about two-thirds of the way down from the top, and as the fall sways back and forth with great variety of motions among these flat-topped pillars, kissing and plashing notes as well as thunder-like detonations are produced, like those of the Yosemite Fall, though on a smaller scale.

The rainbows of the Veil, or rather the spray- and foam-bows, are superb, because the waters are dashed among angular blocks of granite at the foot, producing abundance of spray of the best quality for iris effects, and also for a luxuriant growth of grass and maiden-hair on the side of the talus, which lower down is planted with oak, laurel and willows.

GENERAL FEATURES OF THE VALLEY

On the other side of the Valley, almost immediately opposite the Bridal Veil, there is another fine fall, considerably wider than the Veil when the snow is melting fast and more than 1000 feet in height, measured from the brow of the cliff where it first springs out into the air to the head of the rocky talus on which it strikes and is broken up into ragged cascades. It is called the Ribbon Fall or Virgin's Tears. During the spring floods it is a magnificent object,

[7]

but the suffocating blasts of spray that fill the recess in the wall which it occupies prevent a near approach. In autumn, however, when its feeble current falls in a shower, it may then pass for tears with the sentimental onlooker fresh from a visit to the Bridal Veil.

Just beyond this glorious flood the El Capitan Rock, regarded by many as the most sublime feature of the Valley, is seen through the pine groves, standing forward beyond the general line of the wall in most imposing grandeur, a type of permanence. It is 3300 feet high, a plain, severely simple, glacier-sculptured face of granite, the end of one of the most compact and enduring of the mountain ridges, unrivaled in height and breadth and flawless strength.

Across the Valley from here, next to the Bridal Veil, are the picturesque Cathedral Rocks, nearly 2700 feet high, making a noble display of fine yet massive sculpture. They are closely related to El Capitan, having been eroded from the same mountain ridge by the great Yosemite Glacier when the Valley was in process of formation.

Next to the Cathedral Rocks on the south side towers the Sentinel Rock to a height of more than 3000 feet, a telling monument of the glacial period.

Almost immediately opposite the Sentinel are the Three Brothers, an immense mountain mass with three gables fronting the Valley, one above another, the topmost gable nearly 4000 feet high. They were named for three brothers, sons of old Tenaya, the Yosemite chief, captured here during the Indian War, at the time of the discovery of the Valley in 1852.

Sauntering up the Valley through meadow and grove, in the company of these majestic rocks, which seem to follow us as we advance, gazing, admiring, looking for new wonders ahead where all about us is so wonderful, the thunder of the Yosemite Fall is heard, and when we arrive in front of the Sentinel Rock it is revealed in all its glory from base to summit, half a mile in height, and seeming to spring out into the Valley sunshine direct from the sky. But even this fall, perhaps the most wonderful of its kind in the world, cannot at first hold our attention, for now the wide upper portion of the Valley is displayed to view, with the finely modeled North Dome, the Royal Arches and Washington Column on our left; Glacier Point, with its massive, magnificent sculpture on the right; and in the middle, directly in front, looms Tissiack or Half Dome, the most beautiful and most sublime of all the wonderful Yosemite rocks, rising in serene majesty from flowery groves and meadows to a height of 4750 feet.

THE UPPER CAÑONS

Here the Valley divides into three branches, the Tenaya, Nevada, and Illilouette Cañons, extending back into the fountains of the High Sierra, with scenery every way worthy the relation they bear to Yosemite.

In the south branch, a mile or two from the main Valley, is the Illilouette Fall, 600 feet high, one of the most beautiful of all the Yosemite choir, but to most people inaccessible as yet on account of its rough, steep, boulder-choked cañon. Its principal fountains of ice and snow lie in the beautiful and interesting mountains of the Merced group, while its broad open basin between its fountain mountains and cañon is noted for the beauty of its lakes and forests and magnificent moraines.

Returning to the Valley, and going up the north branch of

Tenaya Cañon, we pass between the North Dome and Half Dome, and in less than an hour come to Mirror Lake, the Dome Cascades, and Tenaya Fall. Beyond the Fall, on the north side of the cañon, is the sublime El Capitan-like rock called Mount Watkins; on the south the vast granite wave of Clouds' Rest, a mile in height; and between them the fine Tenaya Cascade with silvery plumes outspread on smooth glacier-polished folds of granite, making a vertical descent in all of about 700 feet.

Just beyond the Dome Cascades, on the shoulder of Mount Watkins, there is an old trail once used by Indians on their way across the range to Mono, but in the cañon above this point there is no trail of any sort. Between Mount Watkins and Clouds' Rest the cañon is accessible only to mountaineers, and it is so dangerous that I hesitate to advise even good climbers, anxious to test their nerve and skill, to attempt to pass through it. Beyond the Cascades no great difficulty will be encountered. A succession of charming lily gardens and meadows occurs in filled-up lake basins among the rock-waves in the bottom of the cañon, and everywhere the surface of the granite has a smooth-wiped appearance, and in many places reflects the sunbeams like glass, a phenomenon due to glacial action, the cañon having been the channel of one of the main tributaries of the ancient Yosemite Glacier.

About ten miles above the Valley we come to the beautiful Tenaya Lake, and here the cañon terminates. A mile or two above the lake stands the grand Sierra Cathedral, a building of one stone, hewn from the living rock, with sides, roof, gable, spire and ornamental pinnacles, fashioned and finished symmetrically like a work of art, and set on a well-graded plateau about 9000 feet high, as if Nature in making so fine a building had also been careful that it should be finely seen. From every direction its peculiar form and graceful, majestic beauty of expression never fail to charm. Its height from its base to the ridge of the roof is about 2500 feet, and among the pinnacles that adorn the front grand views may be gained of the upper basins of the Merced and Tuolumne Rivers.

Passing the Cathedral we descend into the delightful, spacious Tuolumne Valley, from which excursions may be made to Mounts Dana, Lyell, Ritter, Conness, and Mono Lake, and to the many curious peaks that rise above the meadows on the south, and to the Big Tuolumne Cañon, with its glorious abundance of rocks and falling, gliding, tossing water. For all these the beautiful meadows near the Soda Springs form a delightful center.

NATURAL FEATURES NEAR THE VALLEY

Returning now to Yosemite and ascending the middle or Nevada branch of the Valley, occupied by the main Merced River, we come within a few miles to the Vernal and Nevada Falls, 400 and 600 feet high, pouring their white, rejoicing waters in the midst of the most novel and sublime rock scenery to be found in all the world. Tracing the river beyond the head of the Nevada Fall we are led into the Little Yosemite, a valley like the great Yosemite in form, sculpture and vegetation. It is about three miles long, with walls 1500 to 2000 feet high, cascades coming over them, and the river flowing through the meadows and groves of the level bottom in tranquil, richly-embowered reaches.

Beyond this Little Yosemite in the main cañon, there are three other little yosemites, the highest situated a few miles below the base of Mount Lyell, at an elevation of about 7800 feet above the sea. To describe these, with all their wealth of Yosemite furniture, and the wilderness of lofty peaks above them, the home of the avalanche and treasury of the fountain snow, would take us far beyond the bounds of a single book. Nor can we here consider the formation of these mountain landscapes—how the crystal rocks were brought to light by glaciers made up of crystal snow, making beauty whose influence is so mysterious on every one who sees it.

Of the small glacier lakes so characteristic of these upper regions, there are no fewer than sixty-seven in the basin of the main middle branch, besides countless smaller pools. In the basin of the Illilouette there are sixteen, in the Tenaya basin and its branches thirteen, in the Yosemite Creek basin fourteen, and in the Pohono or Bridal Veil one, making a grand total of one hundred and eleven lakes whose waters come to sing at Yosemite. So glorious is the background of the great Valley, so harmonious its relations to its widespreading fountains.

The same harmony prevails in all the other features of the adjacent landscapes. Climbing out of the Valley by the subordinate cañons, we find the ground rising from the brink of the walls: on the south side to the fountains of the Bridal Veil Creek, the basin of which is noted for the beauty of its meadows and its superb forests of silver fir; on the north side through the basin of the Yosemite Creek to the dividing ridge along the Tuolumne Cañon and the fountains of the Hoffman Range.

DOWN THE YOSEMITE CREEK

In general views the Yosemite Creek basin seems to be paved with domes and smooth, whaleback masses of granite in every stage of development—some showing only their crowns; others rising high and free above the girdling forests, singly or in groups. Others are developed only on one side, forming bold outstanding bosses usually well fringed with shrubs and trees, and presenting the polished surfaces given them by the glacier that brought them into relief. On the upper portion of the basin broad moraine beds have been deposited and on these fine, thrifty forests are growing. Lakes and meadows and small spongy bogs may be found hiding here and there in the woods or back in the fountain recesses of Mount Hoffman, while a thousand gardens are planted along the banks of the streams.

All the wide, fan-shaped upper portion of the basin is covered with a network of small rills that go cheerily on their way to their grand fall in the Valley, now flowing on smooth pavements in sheets thin as glass, now diving under willows and laving their red roots, oozing through green, plushy bogs, plashing over small falls and dancing down slanting cascades, calming again, gliding through patches of smooth glacier meadows with sod of alpine agrostis mixed with blue and white violets and daisies, breaking, tossing among rough boulders and fallen trees, resting in calm pools, flowing together until, all united, they go to their fate with stately, tranquil gestures like a full-grown river. At the crossing of the Mono Trail, about two miles above the head of the Yosemite Fall, the stream is nearly forty feet wide, and when the snow is melting rapidly in the spring it is about four feet deep, with a current of two and a half miles an hour. This is about the volume of water that forms the Fall in May and June when there had been much snow the preceding winter; but it varies greatly from month to month. The snow rapidly vanishes from the open portion of the basin, which faces southward, and only a few of the tributaries reach back to perennial snow and ice fountains in the shadowy amphitheaters on the precipitous northern slopes of Mount Hoffman. The total descent made by the stream from its highest sources to its confluence with the Merced in the Valley is about 6000 feet, while the distance is only about ten miles, an average fall of 600 feet per mile. The last mile of its course lies between the sides of sunken domes and swelling folds of the granite that are clustered and pressed together like a mass of bossy cumulus clouds. Through this shining way Yosemite Creek goes to its fate, swaying and swirling with easy, graceful gestures and singing the last of its mountain songs before it reaches the dizzy edge of Yosemite to fall 2600 feet into another world, where climate, vegetation, inhabitants, all are different. Emerging from this last cañon the stream glides, in flat, lace-like folds, down a smooth incline into a small pool where it seems to rest and compose itself before taking the grand plunge. Then calmly, as if leaving a lake, it slips over the polished lip of the pool down another incline and out over the brow of the precipice in a magnificent curve thick-sown with rainbow spray.

THE YOSEMITE FALL

Long ago before I had traced this fine stream to its head back of Mount Hoffman, I was eager to reach the extreme verge to see how it behaved in flying so far through the air; but after enjoying this view and getting safely away I have never advised any one to follow my steps. The last incline down which the stream journeys so gracefully is so steep and smooth one must slip cautiously forward on hands and feet alongside the rushing water, which so near one's head is very exciting. But to gain a perfect view one must go yet farther, over a curving brow to a slight shelf on the extreme brink. This shelf, formed by the flaking off of a fold of granite, is about three inches wide, just wide enough for a safe rest for one's heels. To me it seemed nerve-trying to slip to this narrow foothold and poise on the edge of such a precipice so close to the confusing whirl of the waters; and after casting longing glances over the shining brow of the fall and listening to its sublime psalm, I concluded not to attempt to go nearer, but, nevertheless, against reasonable judgment, I did. Noticing some tufts of artemisia in a cleft of rock, I filled my mouth with the leaves, hoping their bitter taste might help to keep caution keen and prevent giddiness. In spite of myself I reached the little ledge, got my heels well set, and worked sidewise twenty or thirty feet to a point close to the out-plunging current. Here the view is perfectly free down into the heart of the bright irised throng of comet-like streamers into which the whole ponderous volume of the fall separates, two or three hundred feet below the brow. So glorious a display of pure wildness, acting at close range while cut off from all the world beside, is terribly impressive. A less nerve-trying view may be obtained from a fissured portion of the edge of the cliff about forty yards to the eastward of the fall. Seen from this point towards noon, in the spring, the rainbow on its brow seems to be broken up and mingled with the rushing comets until all the fall is stained with iris colors, leaving no white water visible. This is the best of the safe views from above, the huge steadfast rocks, the flying waters, and the rainbow light forming one of the most glorious pictures conceivable.

The Yosemite Fall is separated into an upper and a lower fall with a series of falls and cascades between them, but when viewed in front from the bottom of the Valley they all appear as one.

So grandly does this magnificent fall display itself from the

floor of the Valley, few visitors take the trouble to climb the walls
to gain nearer views, unable to realize how vastly more impressive
it is near by than at a distance of one or two miles.

A WONDERFUL ASCENT

The views developed in a walk up the zigzags of the trail leading to
the foot of the Upper Fall are about as varied and impressive as
those displayed along the favorite Glacier Point Trail. One rises as
if on wings. The groves, meadows, fern-flats and reaches of the
river gain new interest, as if never seen before; all the views changing in a most striking manner as we go higher from point to point.
The foreground also changes every few rods in the most surprising
manner, although the earthquake talus and the level bench on the
face of the wall over which the trail passes seem monotonous and
commonplace as seen from the bottom of the Valley. Up we climb
with glad exhilaration, through shaggy fringes of laurel, ceanothus, glossy-leaved manzanita and live-oak, from shadow to
shadow across bars and patches of sunshine, the leafy openings
making charming frames for the Valley pictures beheld through
them, and for the glimpses of the high peaks that appear in the
distance. The higher we go the farther we seem to be from the
summit of the vast granite wall. Here we pass a projecting buttress
whose grooved and rounded surface tells a plain story of the time
when the Valley, now filled with sunshine, was filled with ice,
when the grand old Yosemite Glacier, flowing river-like from its
distant fountains, swept through it, crushing, grinding, wearing its
way ever deeper, developing and fashioning these sublime rocks.
Again we cross a white, battered gully, the pathway of rock ava-

The Approach to the Valley

lanches or snow avalanches. Farther on we come to a gentle stream slipping down the face of the cliff in lace-like strips, and dropping from ledge to ledge—too small to be called a fall—trickling, dripping, oozing, a pathless wanderer from one of the upland meadows lying a little way back of the Valley rim, seeking a way century after century to the depths of the Valley without any appreciable channel. Every morning after a cool night, evaporation being checked, it gathers strength and sings like a bird, but as the day advances and the sun strikes its thin currents outspread on the heated precipices, most of its waters vanish ere the bottom of the Valley is reached. Many a fine, hanging-garden aloft on breezy inaccessible heights owes to it its freshness and fullness of beauty; ferneries in shady nooks, filled with Adiantum, Woodwardia, Woodsia, Aspidium, Pellaea, and Cheilanthes, rosetted and tufted and ranged in lines, daintily overlapping, thatching the stupendous cliffs with softest beauty, some of the delicate fronds seeming to float on the warm moist air, without any connection with rock or stream. Nor is there any lack of colored plants wherever they can find a place to cling to; lilies and mints, the showy cardinal mimulus, and glowing cushions of the golden bahia, enlivened with butterflies and bees and all the other small, happy humming creatures that belong to them.

After the highest point on the lower division of the trail is gained it leads up into the deep recess occupied by the great fall, the noblest display of falling water to be found in the Valley, or perhaps in the world. When it first comes in sight it seems almost within reach of one's hand, so great in the spring is its volume and velocity, yet it is still nearly a third of a mile away and appears to recede as we advance. The sculpture of the walls about it is on a scale of grandeur, according nobly with the fall—plain and massive, though elaborately finished, like all the other cliffs about the Valley.

In the afternoon an immense shadow is cast athwart the plateau in front of the fall, and over the chaparral bushes that clothe the slopes and benches of the walls to the eastward, creeping upward until the fall is wholly overcast, the contrast between the shaded and illumined sections being very striking in these near views.

Under this shadow, during the cool centuries immediately following the breaking-up of the Glacial Period, dwelt a small residual glacier, one of the few that lingered on this sun-beaten side of the Valley after the main trunk glacier had vanished. It sent down a long winding current through the narrow cañon on the west side of the fall, and must have formed a striking feature of the ancient scenery of the Valley; the lofty fall of ice and fall of water side by side, yet separate and distinct.

The coolness of the afternoon shadow and the abundant dewy spray make a fine climate for the plateau ferns and grasses, and for the beautiful azalea bushes that grow here in profusion and bloom in September, long after the warmer thickets down on the floor of the Valley have withered and gone to seed. Even close to the fall, and behind it at the base of the cliff, a few venturesome plants may be found undisturbed by the rock-shaking torrent.

The basin at the foot of the fall into which the current directly pours, when it is not swayed by the wind, is about ten feet deep and fifteen to twenty feet in diameter. That it is not much deeper is surprising, when the great height and force of the fall is considered. But the rock where the water strikes probably suffers less erosion than it would were the descent less than half as great, since the current is outspread, and much of its force is spent ere it reaches the bottom—being received on the air as upon an elastic cushion, and borne outward and dissipated over a surface more than fifty yards wide.

This surface, easily examined when the water is low, is intensely clean and fresh looking. It is the raw, quick flesh of the mountain wholly untouched by the weather. In summer droughts, when the snowfall of the preceding winter has been light, the fall is reduced to a mere shower of separate drops without any obscuring spray. Then we may safely go back of it and view the crystal shower from beneath, each drop wavering and pulsing as it makes its way through the air, and flashing off jets of colored light of ravishing beauty. But all this is invisible from the bottom of the Valley, like a thousand other interesting things. One must labor for beauty as for bread, here as elsewhere.

THE GRANDEUR OF THE YOSEMITE FALL

During the time of the spring floods the best near view of the fall is obtained from Fern Ledge on the east side above the blinding spray at a height of about 400 feet above the base of the fall. A climb of about 1400 feet from the Valley has to be made, and there is no trail, but to any one fond of climbing this will make the ascent all the more delightful. A narrow part of the ledge extends to the side of the fall and back of it, enabling us to approach it as closely as we wish. When the afternoon sunshine is streaming through the throng of comets, ever wasting, ever renewed, the marvelous fineness, firmness and variety of their forms are beautifully revealed.

The Yosemite

At the top of the fall they seem to burst forth in irregular spurts from some grand, throbbing mountain heart. Now and then one mighty throb sends forth a mass of solid water into the free air far beyond the others, which rushes alone to the bottom of the fall with long streaming tail, like combed silk, while the others, descending in clusters, gradually mingle and lose their identity. But they all rush past us with amazing velocity and display of power, though apparently drowsy and deliberate in their movements when observed from a distance of a mile or two. The heads of these comet-like masses are composed of nearly solid water, and are dense white in color like pressed snow, from the friction they suffer in rushing through the air, the portion worn off forming the tail, between the white lustrous threads and films of which faint, grayish pencilings appear, while the outer, finer sprays of water-dust, whirling in sunny eddies, are pearly gray throughout. At the bottom of the fall there is but little distinction of form visible. It is mostly a hissing, clashing, seething, upwhirling mass of scud and spray, through which the light sifts in gray and purple tones, while at times when the sun strikes at the required angle, the whole wild and apparently lawless, stormy, striving mass is changed to brilliant rainbow hues, manifesting finest harmony. The middle portion of the fall is the most openly beautiful; lower, the various forms into which the waters are wrought are more closely and voluminously veiled, while higher, towards the head, the current is comparatively simple and undivided. But even at the bottom, in the boiling clouds of spray, there is no confusion, while the rainbow light makes all divine, adding glorious beauty and peace to glorious power. This noble fall has far the richest, as well as the most powerful, voice of all the falls of the Valley, its tones varying from the sharp hiss and rustle of the wind in the glossy leaves of the live-oaks and the soft, sifting, hushing tones of the pines, to the loudest rush and roar of storm winds and thunder among the crags of the summit peaks. The low bass, booming, reverberating tones, heard under favorable circumstances five or six miles away, are formed by the dashing and exploding of heavy masses mixed with air upon two projecting ledges on the face of the cliff, the one on which we are standing and another about 200 feet above it. The torrent of massive comets is continuous at time of high water, while the explosive, booming notes are wildly intermittent, because, unless influenced by the wind, most of the heavier masses shoot out from the face of the precipice, and pass the ledges upon which at other times they are exploded. Occasionally the whole fall is swayed away from the front of the cliff, then suddenly dashed flat against it, or vibrated from side to side like a pendulum, giving rise to endless variety of forms and sounds.

THE NEVADA FALL

The Nevada Fall is 600 feet high and is usually ranked next to the Yosemite in general interest among the five main falls of the Valley. Coming through the Little Yosemite in tranquil reaches, the river is first broken into rapids on a moraine boulder-bar that crosses the lower end of the Valley. Thence it pursues its way to the head of the fall in a rough, solid rock channel, dashing on side angles, heaving in heavy surging masses against elbow knobs, and swirling and swashing in pot-holes without a moment's rest. Thus, already chafed and dashed to foam, overfolded and twisted, it plunges over the brink of the precipice as if glad to escape into the open air. But before it reaches the bottom it is pulverized yet finer by impinging upon a sloping portion of the cliff about half-way down, thus making it the whitest of all the falls of the Valley, and altogether one of the most wonderful in the world.

On the north side, close to its head, a slab of granite projects over the brink, forming a fine point for a view, over its throng of streamers and wild plunging, into its intensely white bosom, and, through the broad drifts of spray, to the river far below, gathering its spent waters and rushing on again down the cañon in glad exultation into Emerald Pool, where at length it grows calm and gets rest for what still lies before it. All the features of the view correspond with the waters in grandeur and wildness. The glacier-sculptured walls of the cañon on either hand, with the sublime mass of the Glacier Point Ridge in front, form a huge triangular pit-like basin, which, filled with the roaring of the falling river, seems as if it might be the hopper of one of the mills of the gods in which the mountains were being ground.

THE VERNAL FALL

The Vernal, about a mile below the Nevada, is 400 feet high, a staid, orderly, graceful, easy-going fall, proper and exact in every movement and gesture, with scarce a hint of the passionate enthusiasm of the Yosemite or of the impetuous Nevada, whose chafed and twisted waters hurrying over the cliff seem glad to escape into the open air, while its deep, booming, thunder-tones reverberate over the listening landscape. Nevertheless it is a favorite with most visitors, doubtless because it is more accessible than any other, more closely approached and better seen and heard. A good stairway ascends the cliff beside it and the level plateau at the head enables one to saunter safely along the edge of the river as it comes from Emerald Pool and to watch its waters, calmly bending over the brow of the precipice, in a sheet eighty feet wide, changing in color from green to purplish gray and white until dashed on a boulder talus. Thence issuing from beneath its fine broad spray-clouds we see the tremendously adventurous river still unspent, beating its way down the wildest and deepest of all its cañons in gray roaring rapids, dear to the ouzel, and below the confluence of the Illilouette, sweeping around the shoulder of the Half Dome on its approach to the head of the tranquil levels of the Valley.

THE ILLILOUETTE FALL

The Illilouette in general appearance most resembles the Nevada. The volume of water is less than half as great, but it is about the same height (600 feet) and its waters receive the same kind of preliminary tossing in a rocky, irregular channel. Therefore it is a very white and fine-grained fall. When it is in full springtime bloom it is partly divided by rocks that roughen the lip of the precipice, but this division amounts only to a kind of fluting and grooving of the column, which has a beautiful effect. It is not nearly so grand a fall as the upper Yosemite, or so symmetrical as the Vernal, or so airily graceful and simple as the Bridal Veil, nor does it ever display so tremendous an outgush of snowy magnificence as the Nevada; but in the exquisite fineness and richness of texture of its flowing folds it surpasses them all.

One of the finest effects of sunlight on falling water I ever saw in Yosemite or elsewhere I found on the brow of this beautiful fall.

The Yosemite

It was in the Indian summer, when the leaf colors were ripe and the great cliffs and domes were transfigured in the hazy golden air. I had scrambled up its rugged talus-dammed cañon, oftentimes stopping to take breath and look back to admire the wonderful views to be had there of the great Half Dome, and to enjoy the extreme purity of the water, which in the motionless pools on this stream is almost perfectly invisible; the colored foliage of the maples, dogwoods, *Rubus* tangles, etc., and the late goldenrods and asters. The voice of the fall was now low, and the grand spring and summer floods had waned to sifting, drifting gauze and thin-broidered folds of linked and arrowy lace-work. When I reached the foot of the fall sunbeams were glinting across its head, leaving all the rest of it in shadow; and on its illumined brow a group of yellow spangles of singular form and beauty were playing, flashing up and dancing in large flame-shaped masses, wavering at times, then steadying, rising and falling in accord with the shifting forms of the water. But the color of the dancing spangles changed not at all. Nothing in clouds or flowers, on bird-wings or the lips of shells, could rival it in fineness. It was the most divinely beautiful mass of rejoicing yellow light I ever beheld—one of Nature's precious gifts that perchance may come to us but once in a lifetime.

THE MINOR FALLS

There are many other comparatively small falls and cascades in the Valley. The most notable are the Yosemite Gorge Fall and Cascades, Tenaya Fall and Cascades, Royal Arch Falls, the two Sentinel Cascades and the falls of Cascade and Tamarack Creeks, a mile or two below the lower end of the Valley. These last are often visited. The others are seldom noticed or mentioned; although in almost any other country they would be visited and described as wonders.

The six intermediate falls in the gorge between the head of the Lower and the base of the Upper Yosemite Falls, separated by a few deep pools and strips of rapids, and three slender, tributary cascades on the west side form a series more strikingly varied and combined than any other in the Valley, yet very few of all the Valley visitors ever see them or hear of them. No available standpoint commands a view of them all. The best general view is obtained from the mouth of the gorge near the head of the Lower Fall. The two lowest of the series, together with one of the three tributary cascades, are visible from this standpoint, but in reaching it the last twenty or thirty feet of the descent is rather dangerous in time of high water, the shelving rocks being then slippery on account of spray, but if one should chance to slip when the water is low, only a bump or two and a harmless plash would be the penalty. No part of the gorge, however, is safe to any but cautious climbers.

Though the dark gorge hall of these rejoicing waters is never flushed by the purple light of morning or evening, it is warmed and cheered by the white light of noonday, which, falling into so much foam and spray of varying degrees of fineness, makes marvelous displays of rainbow colors. So filled, indeed, is it with this precious light, at favorable times it seems to take the place of common air. Laurel bushes shed fragrance into it from above and live-oaks, those fearless mountaineers, hold fast to angular seams and lean out over it with their fringing sprays and bright mirror leaves.

One bird, the ouzel, loves this gorge and flies through it merrily, or cheerily, rather, stopping to sing on foam-washed bosses where other birds could find no rest for their feet. I have even seen a gray squirrel down in the heart of it beside the wild rejoicing water.

One of my favorite night walks was along the rim of this wild gorge in times of high water when the moon was full, to see the lunar bows in the spray.

For about a mile above Mirror Lake the Tenaya Cañon is level, and richly planted with fir, Douglas spruce and libocedrus, forming a remarkably fine grove, at the head of which is the Tenaya Fall. Though seldom seen or described, this is, I think, the most picturesque of all the small falls. A considerable distance above it, Tenaya Creek comes hurrying down, white and foamy, over a flat pavement inclined at an angle of about eighteen degrees. In time of high water this sheet of rapids is nearly seventy feet wide, and is varied in a very striking way by three parallel furrows that extend in the direction of its flow. These furrows, worn by the action of the stream upon cleavage joints, vary in width, are slightly sinuous, and have large boulders firmly wedged in them here and there in narrow places, giving rise, of course, to a complicated series of wild dashes, doublings, and upleaping arches in the swift torrent. Just before it reaches the head of the fall the current is divided, the left division making a vertical drop of about eighty feet in a romantic, leafy, flowery, mossy nook, while the other forms a rugged cascade.

The Royal Arch Fall in time of high water is a magnificent object, forming a broad ornamental sheet in front of the arches. The two Sentinel Cascades, 3000 feet high, are also grand spectacles when the snow is melting fast in the spring, but by the middle of summer they have diminished to mere streaks scarce noticeable amid their sublime surroundings.

The Approach to the Valley

THE BEAUTY OF THE RAINBOWS

The Bridal Veil and Vernal Falls are famous for their rainbows; and special visits to them are often made when the sun shines into the spray at the most favorable angle. But amid the spray and foam and fine-ground mist ever rising from the various falls and cataracts there is an affluence and variety of iris bows scarcely known to visitors who stay only a day or two. Both day and night, winter and summer, this divine light may be seen wherever water is falling, dancing, singing; telling the heart-peace of Nature amid the wildest displays of her power. In the bright spring mornings the black-walled recess at the foot of the Lower Yosemite Fall is lavishly filled with irised spray; and not simply does this span the dashing foam, but the foam itself, the whole mass of it, beheld at a certain distance, seems to be colored, and drifts and wavers from color to color, mingling with the foliage of the adjacent trees, without suggesting any relationship to the ordinary rainbow. This is perhaps the largest and most reservoir-like fountain of iris colors to be found in the Valley.

Lunar rainbows or spray-bows also abound in the glorious affluence of dashing, rejoicing, hurrahing, enthusiastic spring floods, their colors as distinct as those of the sun and regularly and obviously banded, though less vivid. Fine specimens may be found any night at the foot of the Upper Yosemite Fall, glowing gloriously amid the gloomy shadows and thundering waters, whenever there is plenty of moonlight and spray. Even the secondary bow is at times distinctly visible.

The best point from which to observe them is on Fern Ledge. For some time after moonrise, at time of high water, the arc has a span of about five hundred feet, and is set upright; one end planted in the boiling spray at the bottom, the other in the edge of the fall, creeping lower, of course, and becoming less upright as the moon rises higher. This grand arc of color, glowing in mild, shapely beauty in so weird and huge a chamber of night shadows, and amid the rush and roar and tumultuous dashing of this thunder-voiced fall, is one of the most impressive and most cheering of all the blessed mountain evangels.

Smaller bows may be seen in the gorge on the plateau between the Upper and Lower Falls. Once toward midnight, after spending a few hours with the wild beauty of the Upper Fall, I sauntered along the edge of the gorge, looking in here and there, wherever the footing felt safe, to see what I could learn of the night aspects of the smaller falls that dwell there. And down in an exceedingly black, pit-like portion of the gorge, at the foot of the highest of the intermediate falls, into which the moonbeams were pouring through a narrow opening, I saw a well-defined spray-bow, beautifully distinct in colors, spanning the pit from side to side, while pure white foam-waves beneath the beautiful bow were constantly springing up out of the dark into the moonlight like dancing ghosts.

AN UNEXPECTED ADVENTURE

A wild scene, but not a safe one, is made by the moon as it appears through the edge of the Yosemite Fall when one is behind it. Once, after enjoying the night-song of the waters and watching the formation of the colored bow as the moon came round the domes and sent her beams into the wild uproar, I ventured out on the narrow bench that extends back of the fall from Fern Ledge and began to admire the dim-veiled grandeur of the view. I could see the fine gauzy threads of the fall's filmy border by having the light in front; and wishing to look at the moon through the meshes of some of the denser portions of the fall, I ventured to creep farther behind it while it was gently wind-swayed, without taking sufficient thought about the consequences of its swaying back to its natural position after the wind-pressure should be removed. The effect was enchanting: fine, savage music sounding above, beneath, around me; while the moon, apparently in the very midst of the rushing waters, seemed to be struggling to keep her place, on account of the ever-varying form and density of the water masses through which she was seen, now darkly veiled or eclipsed by a rush of thick-headed comets, now flashing out through openings between their tails. I was in fairyland between the dark wall and the wild throng of illumined waters, but suffered sudden disenchantment; for, like the witch-scene in Alloway Kirk, "in an instant all was dark." Down came a dash of spent comets, thin and harmless-looking in the distance, but they felt desperately solid and stony when they struck my shoulders, like a mixture of choking spray and gravel and big hailstones. Instinctively dropping on my knees, I gripped an angle of the rock, curled up like a young fern frond with my face pressed against my breast, and in this attitude submitted as best I could to my thundering bath. The heavier masses seemed to strike like cobblestones, and there was a confused noise of many waters about my ears—hissing, gurgling, clashing sounds that were not heard as music. The situation was quickly realized. How fast one's thoughts burn in such times of stress! I was weighing chances of escape. Would the column be swayed a few inches away from the wall, or would it come yet closer? The fall was in flood and not so lightly would its ponderous mass be swayed. My fate seemed to depend on a breath of the "idle wind." It was moved gently forward, the pounding ceased, and I was once more visited by glimpses of the moon. But fearing I might be caught at a disadvantage in making too hasty a retreat, I moved only a few feet along the bench to where a block of ice lay. I wedged myself between the ice and the wall, and lay face downwards, until the steadiness of the light gave encouragement to rise and get away. Somewhat nerve-shaken, drenched, and benumbed, I made out to build a fire, warmed myself, ran home, reached my cabin before daylight, got an hour or two of sleep, and awoke sound and comfortable, better, not worse, for my hard midnight bath.

CLIMATE AND WEATHER

Owing to the westerly trend of the Valley and its vast depth there is a great difference between the climates of the north and south sides—greater than between many countries far apart; for the south wall is in shadow during the winter months, while the north is bathed in sunshine every clear day. Thus there is mild spring weather on one side of the Valley while winter rules the other. Far up the north-side cliffs many a nook may be found closely embraced by sun-beaten rock-bosses in which flowers bloom every month of the year. Even butterflies may be seen in these high winter gardens except when snow-storms are falling and a few days after they have ceased. Near the head of the lower Yosemite Fall in January I found the ant lions lying in wait in their warm sand-cups, rock ferns being unrolled, club mosses covered with fresh-growing points, the flowers of the laurel nearly open, and the honeysuckle rosetted with bright young leaves; every plant seemed to be thinking about summer. Even on the shadow-side of the Valley the frost is never very sharp. The lowest temperature I ever observed during four winters was 7° Fahrenheit. The first twenty-four days of January had an average temperature at 9 A.M. of 32°, minimum 22°; at 3 P.M. the average was 40° 30', the minimum 32°. Along the top of the walls, 7000 and 8000 feet high, the temperature was, of course, much lower. But the difference in temperature between the north and south sides is due not so much to the winter sunshine as to the heat of the preceding summer, stored up in the rocks, which rapidly melts the snow in contact with them. For though summer sun-heat is stored in the rocks of the south side also, the amount is much less because the rays fall obliquely on the south wall even in summer and almost vertically on the north.

The upper branches of the Yosemite streams are buried every winter beneath a heavy mantle of snow, and set free in the spring in magnificent floods. Then, all the fountains, full and overflowing, every living thing breaks forth into singing, and the glad exulting streams, shining and falling in the warm sunny weather, shake everything into music, making all the mountain-world a song.

The great annual spring thaw usually begins in May in the forest region, and in June and July on the high Sierra, varying somewhat both in time and fullness with the weather and the depth of the snow. Toward the end of summer the streams are at their lowest ebb, few even of the strongest singing much above a whisper as they slip and ripple through gravel and boulder-beds from pool to pool in the hollows of their channels, and drop in pattering showers like rain, and slip down precipices and fall in sheets of embroidery, fold over fold. But, however low their singing, it is always ineffably fine in tone, in harmony with the restful time of the year.

The first snow of the season that comes to the help of the streams usually falls in September or October, sometimes even in the latter part of August, in the midst of yellow Indian summer, when the goldenrods and gentians of the glacier meadows are in their prime. This Indian-summer snow, however, soon melts, the chilled flowers spread their petals to the sun, and the gardens as well as the streams are refreshed as if only a warm shower had fallen. The snow-storms that load the mountains to form the main fountain supply for the year seldom set in before the middle or end of November.

WINTER BEAUTY OF THE VALLEY

When the first heavy storms stopped work on the high mountains, I made haste down to my Yosemite den, not to "hole up" and sleep the white months away; I was out every day, and often all night, sleeping but little, studying the so-called wonders and common things ever on show, wading, climbing, sauntering among the blessed storms and calms, rejoicing in almost everything alike that I could see or hear: the glorious brightness of frosty mornings; the sunbeams pouring over the white domes and crags into the groves and waterfalls, kindling marvelous iris fires in the hoarfrost and spray; the great forests and mountains in their deep noon sleep; the good-night alpenglow; the stars; the solemn gazing moon, drawing the huge domes and headlands one by one glowing white out of the shadows hushed and breathless like an audience in awful enthusiasm, while the meadows at their feet sparkle with frost-stars

The Approach to the Valley

like the sky; the sublime darkness of storm-nights, when all the lights are out; the clouds in whose depths the frail snow-flowers grow; the behavior and many voices of the different kinds of storms, trees, birds, waterfalls, and snow-avalanches in the ever-changing weather.

Every clear, frosty morning loud sounds are heard booming and reverberating from side to side of the Valley at intervals of a few minutes, beginning soon after sunrise and continuing an hour or two like a thunder-storm. In my first winter in the Valley I could not make out the source of this noise. I thought of falling boulders, rock-blasting, etc. Not till I saw what looked like hoarfrost dropping from the side of the Fall was the problem explained. The strange thunder is made by the fall of sections of ice formed of spray that is frozen on the face of the cliff along the sides of the Upper Yosemite Fall—a sort of crystal plaster, a foot or two thick, cracked off by the sunbeams, awakening all the Valley like cock-crowing, announcing the finest weather, shouting aloud Nature's infinite industry and love of hard work in creating beauty.

EXPLORING AN ICE CONE

This frozen spray gives rise to one of the most interesting winter features of the Valley—a cone of ice at the foot of the fall, four or five hundred feet high. From the Fern Ledge standpoint its crater-like throat is seen, down which the fall plunges with deep, gasping explosions of compressed air, and, after being well churned in the stormy interior, the water bursts forth through arched openings at its base, apparently scourged and weary and glad to escape, while belching spray, spouted up out of the throat past the descending current, is wafted away in irised drifts to the adjacent rocks and groves. It is built during the night and early hours of the morning; only in spells of exceptionally cold and cloudy weather is the work continued through the day. The greater part of the spray material falls in crystalline showers direct to its place, something like a small local snow-storm; but a considerable portion is first frozen on the face of the cliff along the sides of the fall and stays there until expanded and cracked off in irregular masses, some of them tons in weight, to be built into the walls of the cone; while in windy, frosty weather, when the fall is swayed from side to side, the cone is well drenched and the loose ice masses and spray-dust are all firmly welded and frozen together. Thus the finest of the downy wafts and curls of spray-dust, which in mild nights fall about as silently as dew, are held back until sunrise to make a store of heavy ice to reinforce the waterfall's thunder-tones.

While the cone is in process of formation, growing higher and wider in the frosty weather, it looks like a beautiful smooth, pure-white hill; but when it is wasting and breaking up in the spring its surface is strewn with leaves, pine branches, stones, sand, etc., that have been brought over the fall, making it look like a heap of avalanche detritus.

Anxious to learn what I could about the structure of this curious hill I often approached it in calm weather and tried to climb it, carrying an ax to cut steps. Once I nearly succeeded in gaining the summit. At the base I was met by a current of spray and wind that made seeing and breathing difficult. I pushed on backward, however, and soon gained the slope of the hill, where by creeping close to the surface most of the choking blast passed over me and I managed to crawl up with but little difficulty. Thus I made my way nearly to the summit, halting at times to peer up through the wild whirls of spray at the veiled grandeur of the fall, or to listen to the thunder beneath me; the whole hill was sounding as if it were a huge, bellowing drum. I hoped that by waiting until the fall was blown aslant I should be able to climb to the lip of the crater and get a view of the interior; but a suffocating blast, half air, half water, followed by the fall of an enormous mass of frozen spray from a spot high up on the wall, quickly discouraged me. The whole cone was jarred by the blow and some fragments of the mass sped past me dangerously near; so I beat a hasty retreat, chilled and drenched, and lay down on a sunny rock to dry.

Once during a wind-storm when I saw that the fall was frequently blown westward, leaving the cone dry, I ran up to Fern Ledge hoping to gain a clear view of the interior. I set out at noon. All the way up the storm notes were so loud about me that the voice of the fall was almost drowned by them. Notwithstanding the rocks and bushes everywhere were drenched by the wind-driven spray, I approached the brink of the precipice overlooking the mouth of the ice cone, but I was almost suffocated by the drenching, gusty spray, and was compelled to seek shelter. I searched for some hiding-place in the wall from whence I might run out at some opportune moment when the fall with its whirling spray and torn shreds of comet tails and trailing, tattered skirts was borne westward, as I had seen it carried several times before, leaving the cliffs on the east side and the ice hill bare in the sunlight. I had not long to wait, for, as if ordered so for my special accommodation, the mighty downrush of comets with their whirling drapery swung westward and remained aslant for nearly half an hour. The cone was admirably lighted and deserted by the water, which fell most of the time on the rocky western slopes mostly outside of the cone. The mouth into which the fall pours was, as near as I could guess, about one hundred feet in diameter north and south and about two hundred feet east and west, which is about the shape and size of the fall at its best in its normal condition at this season.

The crater-like opening was not a true oval, but more like a huge coarse mouth. I could see down the throat about one hundred feet or perhaps farther.

The fall precipice overhangs from a height of 400 feet above the base; therefore the water strikes some distance from the base of the cliff, allowing space for the accumulation of a considerable mass of ice between the fall and the wall.

2

Winter Storms and Spring Floods

THE Bridal Veil and the Upper Yosemite Falls, on account of their height and exposure, are greatly influenced by winds. The common summer winds that come up the river cañon from the plains are seldom very strong; but the north winds do some very wild work, worrying the falls and the forests, and hanging snow-banners on the comet-peaks. One wild winter morning I was awakened by a storm-wind that was playing with the falls as if they were mere wisps of mist and making the great pines bow and sing with glorious enthusiasm. The Valley had been visited a short time before by a series of fine snow-storms, and the floor and the cliffs and all the region round about were lavishly adorned with its best winter jewelry, the air was full of fine snow-dust, and pine branches, tassels and empty cones were flying in an almost continuous flock.

Soon after sunrise, when I was seeking a place safe from flying branches, I saw the Lower Yosemite Fall thrashed and pulverized from top to bottom into one glorious mass of rainbow dust; while a thousand feet above it the main Upper Fall was suspended on the face of the cliff in the form of an inverted bow, all silvery white and fringed with short wavering strips. Then, suddenly assailed by a tremendous blast, the whole mass of the fall was blown into threads and ribbons, and driven back over the brow of the cliff whence it came, as if denied admission to the Valley. This kind of storm-work was continued about ten or fifteen minutes; then another change in the play of the huge exulting swirls and billows and upheaving domes of the gale allowed the baffled fall to gather and arrange its tattered waters, and sink down again in its place. As the day advanced, the gale gave no sign of dying, excepting brief lulls, the Valley was filled with its weariless roar, and the cloudless sky grew garish-white from myriads of minute, sparkling snow-spicules. In the afternoon, while I watched the Upper Fall from the shelter of a big pine tree, it was suddenly arrested in its descent at a point about half-way down, and was neither blown upward nor driven aside, but simply held stationary in mid-air, as if gravitation below that point in the path of its descent had ceased to act. The ponderous flood, weighing hundreds of tons, was sustained, hovering, hesitating, like a bunch of thistledown, while I counted one hundred and ninety. All this time the ordinary amount of water was coming over the cliff and accumulating in the air, swedging and widening and forming an irregular cone about seven hundred feet high, tapering to the top of the wall, the whole standing still, resting on the invisible arm of the North Wind. At length, as if commanded to go on again, scores of arrowy comets shot forth from the bottom of the suspended mass as if escaping from separate outlets.

The brow of El Capitan was decked with long snow-streamers like hair, Clouds' Rest was fairly enveloped in drifting gossamer films, and the Half Dome loomed up in the garish light like a majestic, living creature clad in the same gauzy, wind-woven drapery, while upward currents meeting at times overhead made it smoke like a volcano.

Winter Storms and Spring Floods

AN EXTRAORDINARY STORM AND FLOOD

Glorious as are these rocks and waters arrayed in storm robes, or chanting rejoicing in every-day dress, they are still more glorious when rare weather conditions meet to make them sing with floods. Only once during all the years I have lived in the Valley have I seen it in full flood bloom. In 1871 the early winter weather was delightful; the days all sunshine, the nights all starry and calm, calling forth fine crops of frost-crystals on the pines and withered ferns and grasses for the morning sunbeams to sift through. In the afternoon of December 16, when I was sauntering on the meadows, I noticed a massive crimson cloud growing in solitary grandeur above the Cathedral Rocks, its form scarcely less striking than its color. It had a picturesque, bulging base like an old sequoia, a smooth, tapering stem, and a bossy, down-curling crown like a mushroom; all its parts were colored alike, making one mass of translucent crimson. Wondering what the meaning of that strange, lonely red cloud might be, I was up betimes next morning looking at the weather, but all seemed tranquil as yet. Towards noon gray clouds with a close, curly grain like bird's-eye maple began to grow, and late at night rain fell, which soon changed to snow. Next morning the snow on the meadows was about ten inches deep, and it was still falling in a fine, cordial storm. During the night of the 18th heavy rain fell on the snow, but as the temperature was 34°, the snow-line was only a few hundred feet above the bottom of the Valley, and one had only to climb a little higher than the tops of the pines to get out of the rain-storm into the snow-storm. The streams, instead of being increased in volume by the storm, were diminished, because the snow sponged up part of their waters and choked the smaller tributaries. But about midnight the temperature suddenly rose to 42°, carrying the snow-line far beyond the Valley walls, and next morning Yosemite was rejoicing in a glorious flood. The comparatively warm rain falling on the snow was at first absorbed and held back, and so also was that portion of the snow that the rain melted, and all that was melted by the warm wind, until the whole mass of snow was saturated and became sludgy, and at length slipped and rushed simultaneously from a thousand slopes in wildest extravagance, heaping and swelling flood over flood, and plunging into the Valley in stupendous avalanches.

Awakened by the roar, I looked out and at once recognized the extraordinary character of the storm. The rain was still pouring in torrent abundance and the wind at gale speed was doing all it could with the flood-making rain.

The section of the north wall visible from my cabin was fairly streaked with new falls—wild roaring singers that seemed strangely out of place. Eager to get into the midst of the show, I snatched a piece of bread for breakfast and ran out. The mountain waters, suddenly liberated, seemed to be holding a grand jubilee. The two Sentinel Cascades rivaled the great falls at ordinary stages, and across the Valley by the Three Brothers I caught glimpses of more falls than I could readily count; while the whole Valley throbbed and trembled, and was filled with an awful, massive, solemn, sea-like roar. After gazing a while enchanted with the network of new falls that were adorning and transfiguring every rock in sight, I tried to reach the upper meadows, where the Valley is widest, that I might be able to see the walls on both sides, and thus gain general views. But the river was over its banks and the meadows were flooded, forming an almost continuous lake dotted with blue sludgy islands, while innumerable streams roared like lions across my path and were sweeping forward rocks and logs with tremendous energy over ground where tiny gilias had been growing but a short time before. Climbing into the talus slopes, where these savage torrents were broken among earthquake boulders, I managed to cross them, and force my way up the Valley to Hutchings' Bridge, where I crossed the river and waded to the middle of the upper meadow. Here most of the new falls were in sight, probably the most glorious assemblage of waterfalls ever displayed from any one standpoint. On that portion of the south wall between Hutchings' and the Sentinel there were ten falls plunging and booming from a height of nearly three thousand feet, the smallest of which might have been heard miles away. In the neighborhood of Glacier Point there were six; between the Three Brothers and Yosemite Fall, nine; between Yosemite and Royal Arch Falls, ten; from Washington Column to Mount Watkins, ten; on the slopes of Half Dome and Clouds' Rest, facing Mirror Lake and Tenaya Cañon, eight; on the shoulder of Half Dome, facing the Valley, three: fifty-six new falls occupying the upper end of the Valley, besides a countless host of silvery threads gleaming everywhere. In all the Valley there must have been upwards of a hundred. As if celebrating some great event, falls and cascades in Yosemite costume were coming down everywhere from fountain basins, far and near; and, though newcomers, they behaved and sang as if they had lived here always.

All summer-visitors will remember the comet forms of the Yosemite Fall and the laces of the Bridal Veil and Nevada. In the falls of this winter jubilee the lace forms predominated, but there was no lack of thunder-toned comets. The lower portion of one of the Sentinel Cascades was composed of two main white torrents with the space between them filled in with chained and beaded gauze of intricate pattern, through the singing threads of which the purplish-gray rock could be dimly seen. The series above Glacier Point was still more complicated in structure, displaying every form that one could imagine water might be dashed and combed and woven into. Those on the north wall between Washington Column and the Royal Arch Fall were so nearly related they formed an almost continuous sheet, and these again were but slightly separated from those about Indian Cañon. The group about the Three Brothers and El Capitan, owing to the topography and cleavage of the cliffs back of them, was more broken and irregular. The Tissiack Cascades were comparatively small, yet sufficient to give that noblest of mountain rocks a glorious voice. In the midst of all this extravagant rejoicing the great Yosemite Fall was scarce heard until about three o'clock in the afternoon. Then I was startled by a sudden thundering crash as if a rock avalanche had come to the help of the roaring waters. This was the flood-wave of Yosemite Creek, which had just arrived, delayed by the distance it had to travel, and by the choking snows of its widespread fountains. Now, with volume tenfold increased beyond its springtime fullness, it took its place as leader of the glorious choir.

And the winds, too, were singing in wild accord, playing on every tree and rock, surging against the huge brows and domes and outstanding battlements, deflected hither and thither and broken into a thousand cascading, roaring currents in the cañons, and low bass, drumming swirls in the hollows. And these again, reacting on the clouds, eroded immense cavernous spaces in their gray depths and swept forward the resulting detritus in ragged trains like

the moraines of glaciers. These cloud movements in turn published the work of the winds, giving them a visible body, and enabling us to trace them. As if endowed with independent motion,
a detached cloud would rise hastily to the very top of the wall as if
on some important errand, examining the faces of the cliffs, and
then perhaps as suddenly descend to sweep imposingly along the
meadows, trailing its draggled fringes through the pines, fondling
the waving spires with infinite gentleness, or, gliding behind a
grove or a single tree, bringing it into striking relief, as it bowed and
waved in solemn rhythm. Sometimes, as the busy clouds drooped
and condensed or dissolved to misty gauze, half of the Valley
would be suddenly veiled, leaving here and there some lofty head-
land cut off from all visible connection with the walls, looming
alone, dim, spectral, as if belonging to the sky—visitors, like the
new falls, come to take part in the glorious festival. Thus for two
days and nights in measureless extravagance the storm went on,
and mostly without spectators, at least of a terrestrial kind. I saw
nobody out—bird, bear, squirrel, or man. Tourists had vanished
months before, and the hotel people and laborers were out of sight,
careful about getting cold, and satisfied with views from windows.
The bears, I suppose, were in their cañon-boulder dens, the squirrels in their knot-hole nests, the grouse in close fir groves, and the
small singers in the Indian Cañon chaparral, trying to keep warm
and dry. Strange to say, I did not see even the water-ouzels, though
they must have greatly enjoyed the storm.

This was the most sublime waterfall flood I ever saw—clouds,
winds, rocks, waters, throbbing together as one. And then to con-
template what was going on simultaneously with all this in other
mountain temples; the Big Tuolumne Cañon—how the white

waters and the winds were singing there! And in Hetch Hetchy Valley and the great King's River yosemite, and in all the other Sierra cañons and valleys from Shasta to the southernmost fountains of the Kern, thousands of rejoicing flood waterfalls chanting together in jubilee dress.

3

Snow-Storms

As has been already stated, the first of the great snow-storms that
replenish the Yosemite fountains seldom sets in before the end of
November. Then, warned by the sky, wide-awake mountaineers,
together with the deer and most of the birds, make haste to the
lowlands or foothills; and burrowing marmots, mountain beavers,
wood-rats, and other small mountain people, go into winter quar-
ters, some of them not again to see the light of day until the general
awakening and resurrection of the spring in June or July. The fertile clouds, drooping and condensing in brooding silence, seem to
be thoughtfully examining the forests and streams with reference
to the work that lies before them. At length, all their plans per-
fected, tufted flakes and single starry crystals come in sight, sol-
emnly swirling and glinting to their blessed appointed places; and
soon the busy throng fills the sky and makes darkness like night.
The first heavy fall is usually from about two to four feet in depth;
then with intervals of days or weeks of bright weather storm succeeds storm, heaping snow on snow, until thirty to fifty feet has
fallen. But on account of its settling and compacting, and waste
from melting and evaporation, the average depth actually found at
any time seldom exceeds ten feet in the forest regions, or fifteen
feet along the slopes of the summit peaks. After snow-storms come
avalanches, varying greatly in form, size, behavior and in the songs
they sing; some on the smooth slopes of the mountains are short

and broad; others long and river-like in the side cañons of yosemites and in the main cañons, flowing in regular channels and
booming like waterfalls, while countless smaller ones fall everywhere from laden trees and rocks and lofty cañon walls. Most delightful it is to stand in the middle of Yosemite on still clear
mornings after snow-storms and watch the throng of avalanches as
they come down, rejoicing, to their places, whispering, thrilling
like birds, or booming and roaring like thunder. The noble yellow
pines stand hushed and motionless as if under a spell until the
morning sunshine begins to sift through their laden spires; then the
dense masses on the ends of the leafy branches begin to shift and
fall, those from the upper branches striking the lower ones in
succession, enveloping each tree in a hollow conical avalanche of
fairy fineness; while the relieved branches spring up and wave with
startling effect in the general stillness, as if each tree was moving of
its own volition. Hundreds of broad cloud-shaped masses may also
be seen, leaping over the brows of the cliffs from great heights,
descending at first with regular avalanche speed until, worn into
dust by friction, they float in front of the precipices like irised
clouds. Those which descend from the brow of El Capitan are
particularly fine; but most of the great Yosemite avalanches flow in
regular channels like cascades and waterfalls. When the snow first
gives way on the upper slopes of their basins, a dull rushing, rumbling sound is heard which rapidly increases and seems to draw
nearer with appalling intensity of tone. Presently the white flood
comes bounding into sight over bosses and sheer places, leaping
from bench to bench, spreading and narrowing and throwing off
clouds of whirling dust like the spray of foaming cataracts. Compared with waterfalls and cascades, avalanches are short-lived, few

of them lasting more than a minute or two, and the sharp, clashing sounds so common in falling water are mostly wanting; but in their low massy thundertones and purple-tinged whiteness, and in their dress, gait, gestures and general behavior, they are much alike.

AVALANCHES

Besides these common after-storm avalanches that are to be found not only in the Yosemite but in all the deep, sheer-walled cañons of the Range there are two other important kinds, which may be called annual and century avalanches, which still further enrich the scenery. The only place about the Valley where one may be sure to see the annual kind is on the north slope of Clouds' Rest. They are composed of heavy, compacted snow, which has been subjected to frequent alternations of freezing and thawing. They are developed on cañon and mountain-sides at an elevation of from nine to ten thousand feet, where the slopes are inclined at an angle too low to shed off the dry winter snow, and which accumulates until the spring thaws sap their foundations and make them slippery; then away in grand style go the ponderous icy masses without any fine snow-dust. Those of Clouds' Rest descend like thunderbolts for more than a mile.

The great century avalanches and the kind that mow wide swaths through the upper forests occur on mountain-sides about ten or twelve thousand feet high, where under ordinary weather conditions the snow accumulated from winter to winter lies at rest for many years, allowing trees, fifty to a hundred feet high, to grow undisturbed on the slopes beneath them. On their way down through the woods they seldom fail to make a perfectly clean sweep, stripping off the soil as well as the trees, clearing paths two or three hundred yards wide from the timber line to the glacier meadows or lakes, and piling their uprooted trees, head downward, in rows along the sides of the gaps like lateral moraines. Scars and broken branches of the trees standing on the sides of the gaps record the depth of the overwhelming flood; and when we come to count the annual wood-rings on the uprooted trees we learn that some of these immense avalanches occur only once in a century or even at still wider intervals.

A RIDE ON AN AVALANCHE

Few Yosemite visitors ever see snow avalanches and fewer still know the exhilaration of riding on them. In all my mountaineering I have enjoyed only one avalanche ride, and the start was so sudden and the end came so soon I had but little time to think of the danger that attends this sort of travel, though at such times one thinks fast. One fine Yosemite morning after a heavy snowfall, being eager to see as many avalanches as possible and wide views of the forest and summit peaks in their new white robes before the sunshine had time to change them, I set out early to climb by a side cañon to the top of a commanding ridge a little over three thousand feet above the Valley. On account of the looseness of the snow that blocked the cañon I knew the climb would require a long time, some three or four hours as I estimated; but it proved far more difficult than I had anticipated. Most of the way I sank waist deep, almost out of sight in some places. After spending the whole day to within half an hour or so of sundown, I was still several hundred feet below the summit. Then my hopes were reduced to getting up in time to see the sunset. But I was not to get summit views of any sort that day, for deep trampling near the cañon head, where the snow was strained, started an avalanche, and I was swished down to the foot of the cañon as if by enchantment. The wallowing ascent had taken nearly all day, the descent only about a minute. When the avalanche started I threw myself on my back and spread my arms to try to keep from sinking. Fortunately, though the grade of the cañon is very steep, it is not interrupted by precipices large enough to cause outbounding or free plunging. On no part of the rush was I buried. I was only moderately imbedded on the surface or at times a little below it, and covered with a veil of back-streaming dust particles; and as the whole mass beneath and about me joined in the flight there was no friction, though I was tossed here and there and lurched from side to side. When the avalanche swedged and came to rest I found myself on top of the crumpled pile without a bruise or scar. This was a fine experience. Hawthorne says somewhere that steam has spiritualized travel; though unspiritual smells, smoke, etc., still attend steam travel. This flight in what might be called a milky way of snow-stars was the most spiritual and exhilarating of all the modes of motion I have ever experienced. Elijah's flight in a chariot of fire could hardly have been more gloriously exciting.

THE STREAMS IN OTHER SEASONS

In the spring, after all the avalanches are down and the snow is melting fast, then all the Yosemite streams, from their fountains to their falls, sing their grandest songs. Countless rills make haste to the rivers, running and singing soon after sunrise, louder and louder with increasing volume until sundown; then they gradually fail through the frosty hours of the night. In this way the volume of the upper branches of the river is nearly doubled during the day, rising and falling as regularly as the tides of the sea. Then the Merced overflows its banks, flooding the meadows, sometimes almost from wall to wall in some places, beginning to rise towards sundown just when the streams on the fountains are beginning to diminish, the difference in time of the daily rise and fall being caused by the distance the upper flood streams have to travel before reaching the Valley. In the warmest weather they seem fairly to shout for joy and clash their upleaping waters together like clapping of hands; racing down the cañons with white manes flying in glorious exuberance of strength, compelling huge, sleeping boulders to wake up and join in their dance and song, to swell their exulting chorus.

In early summer, after the flood season, the Yosemite streams are in their prime, running crystal clear, deep and full but not overflowing their banks—about as deep through the night as the day, the difference in volume so marked in spring being now too slight to be noticed. Nearly all the weather is cloudless and everything is at its brightest—lake, river, garden and forest with all their life. Most of the plants are in full flower. The blessed ouzels have built their mossy huts and are now singing their best songs with the streams.

In tranquil, mellow autumn, when the year's work is about done and the fruits are ripe, birds and seeds out of their nests, and all the landscape is glowing like a benevolent countenance, then the streams are at their lowest ebb, with scarce a memory left of their wild spring floods. The small tributaries that do not reach

Snow-Storms

back to the lasting snow fountains of the summit peaks shrink to whispering, tinkling currents. After the snow is gone from the basins, excepting occasional thunder-showers, they are now fed only by small springs whose waters are mostly evaporated in passing over miles of warm pavements, and in feeling their way slowly from pool to pool through the midst of boulders and sand. Even the main rivers are so low they may easily be forded, and their grand falls and cascades, now gentle and approachable, have waned to sheets of embroidery.

4

Snow Banners

BUT it is on the mountain tops, when they are laden with loose, dry snow and swept by a gale from the north, that the most magnificent storm scenery is displayed. The peaks along the axis of the Range are then decorated with resplendent banners, some of them more than a mile long, shining, streaming, waving with solemn exuberant enthusiasm as if celebrating some surpassingly glorious event.

The snow of which these banners are made falls on the high Sierra in most extravagant abundance, sometimes to a depth of fifteen or twenty feet, coming from the fertile clouds not in large tangled flakes such as one oftentimes sees in Yosemite, seldom even in complete crystals, for many of the starry blossoms fall before they are ripe, while most of those that attain perfect development as six-petaled flowers are more or less broken by glinting and chafing against one another on the way down to their work. This dry frosty snow is prepared for the grand banner-waving celebrations by the action of the wind. Instead of at once finding rest like that which falls into the tranquil depths of the forest, it is shoved and rolled and beaten against boulders and out-jutting rocks, swirled in pits and hollows like sand in river pot-holes, and ground into sparkling dust. And when storm winds find this snow-dust in a loose condition on the slopes above the timber-line they toss it back into the sky and sweep it onward from peak to peak in the form of smooth regular banners, or in cloudy drifts, according to the velocity and direction of the wind, and the conformation of the slopes over which it is driven. While thus flying through the air a small portion escapes from the mountains to the sky as vapor; but far the greater part is at length locked fast in bossy overcurling cornices along the ridges, or in stratified sheets in the glacier cirques, some of it to replenish the small residual glaciers and remain silent and rigid for centuries before it is finally melted and sent singing down home to the sea.

But, though snow-dust and storm-winds abound on the mountains, regular shapely banners are, for causes we shall presently see, seldom produced. During the five winters that I spent in Yosemite I made many excursions to high points above the walls in all kinds of weather to see what was going on outside; from all my lofty outlooks I saw only one banner-storm that seemed in every way perfect. This was in the winter of 1873, when the snow-laden peaks were swept by a powerful norther. I was awakened early in the morning by a wild storm-wind and of course I had to make haste to the middle of the Valley to enjoy it. Rugged torrents and avalanches from the main wind-flood overhead were roaring down the side cañons and over the cliffs, arousing the rocks and the trees and the streams alike into glorious hurrahing enthusiasm, shaking the whole Valley into one huge song. Yet inconceivable as it must seem even to those who love all Nature's wildness, the storm was telling its story on the mountains in still grander characters.

A WONDERFUL WINTER SCENE

I had long been anxious to study some points in the structure of the ice-hill at the foot of the Upper Yosemite Fall, but, as I have already explained, blinding spray had hitherto prevented me from getting sufficiently near it. This morning the entire body of the Fall was oftentimes torn into gauzy strips and blown horizontally along the face of the cliff, leaving the ice-hill dry; and while making my way to the top of Fern Ledge to seize so favorable an opportunity to look down its throat, the peaks of the Merced group came in sight over the shoulder of the South Dome, each waving a white glowing banner against the dark blue sky, as regular in form and firm and fine in texture as if it were made of silk. So rare and splendid a picture, of course, smothered everything else and I at once began to scramble and wallow up the snow-choked Indian Cañon to a ridge about 8000 feet high, commanding a general view of the main summits along the axis of the Range, feeling assured I should find them bannered still more gloriously; nor was I in the least disappointed. I reached the top of the ridge in four or five hours, and through an opening in the woods the most imposing wind-storm effect I ever beheld came full in sight; unnumbered mountains rising sharply into the cloudless sky, their bases solid white, their sides plashed with snow, like ocean rocks with foam, and on every summit a magnificent silvery banner, from two thousand to six thousand feet in length, slender at the point of attachment, and widening gradually until about a thousand or fifteen hundred feet in breadth, and as shapely and as substantial looking in texture as the banners of the finest silk, all streaming and waving free and clear in the sun-glow with nothing to blur the sublime picture they made.

Fancy yourself standing beside me on this Yosemite Ridge. There is a strange garish glitter in the air and the gale drives wildly overhead, but you feel nothing of its violence, for you are looking out through a sheltered opening in the woods, as through a window. In the immediate foreground there is a forest of silver firs, their foliage warm yellow-green, and the snow beneath them is strewn with their plumes, plucked off by the storm; and beyond a broad, ridgy, cañon-furrowed, dome-dotted middle ground, darkened here and there with belts of pines, you behold the lofty snow-laden mountains in glorious array, waving their banners with jubilant enthusiasm as if shouting aloud for joy. They are twenty miles away, but you would not wish them nearer, for every feature is distinct, and the whole wonderful show is seen in its right proportions, like a painting on the sky.

And now after this general view, mark how sharply the ribs and buttresses and summits of the mountains are defined, excepting the portions veiled by the banners; how gracefully and nobly the banners are waving in accord with the throbbing of the wind-flood; how trimly each is attached to the very summit of its peak like a streamer at a mast-head; how bright and glowing white they are, and how finely their fading fringes are penciled on the sky! See how solid white and opaque they are at the point of attachment and how filmy and translucent toward the end, so that the parts of the peaks past which they are streaming look dim as if seen through a veil of ground glass. And see how some of the longest of the banners on the highest peaks are streaming perfectly free from peak to peak across intervening notches or passes, while others overlap and partly hide one another.

As to their formation, we find that the main causes of the wondrous beauty and perfection of those we are looking at are the favorable direction and force of the wind, the abundance of snow-dust, and the form of the north sides of the peaks. In general, the north sides are concave in both their horizontal and vertical sections, having been sculptured into this shape by the residual glaciers that lingered in the protecting northern shadows, while the sun-beaten south sides, having never been subjected to this kind of glaciation, are convex or irregular. It is essential, therefore, not only that the wind should move with great velocity and steadiness to supply a sufficiently copious and continuous stream of snow-dust, but that it should come from the north. No perfect banner is ever hung on the Sierra peaks by the south wind. Had the gale to-day blown from the south, leaving the other conditions unchanged, only swirling, interfering, cloudy drifts would have been produced; for the snow, instead of being spouted straight up and over the tops of the peaks in condensed currents to be drawn out as streamers, would have been driven over the convex southern slopes from peak to peak like white pearly fog.

It appears, therefore, that shadows in great part determine not only the forms of lofty ice mountains, but also those of the snow banners that the wild winds hang upon them.

EARTHQUAKE STORMS

The avalanche taluses, leaning against the walls at intervals of a mile or two, are among the most striking and interesting of the secondary features of the Valley. They are from about three to five hundred feet high, made up of huge, angular, well-preserved, unshifting boulders, and instead of being slowly weathered from the cliffs like ordinary taluses, they were all formed suddenly and simultaneously by a great earthquake that occurred at least three centuries ago. And though thus hurled into existence in a few seconds or minutes, they are the least changeable of all the Sierra soil-beds. Excepting those which were launched directly into the channels of swift rivers, scarcely one of their wedged and interlacing boulders has moved since the day of their creation; and though mostly made up of huge blocks of granite, many of them from ten to fifty feet cube, weighing thousands of tons with only a few small chips, trees and shrubs make out to live and thrive on them and even delicate herbaceous plants—draperia, collomia, zauschneria, etc., soothing and coloring their wild rugged slopes with gardens and groves.

I was long in doubt on some points concerning the origin of these taluses. Plainly enough they were derived from the cliffs above them, because they are of the size of scars on the wall, the rough angular surface of which contrasts with the rounded, glaciated, unfractured parts. It was plain, too, that instead of being made up of material slowly and gradually weathered from the cliffs like ordinary taluses, almost every one of them had been formed suddenly in a single avalanche, and had not been increased in size during the last three or four centuries, for trees three or four hundred years old are growing on them, some standing at the top close to the wall without a bruise or broken branch, showing that scarcely a single boulder had ever fallen among them. Furthermore, all these taluses throughout the Range seemed by the trees and lichens growing on them to be of the same age. All the phenomena thus pointed straight to a grand ancient earthquake. But for years I left the question open, and went on from cañon to cañon, observing again and again; measuring the heights of taluses throughout the Range on both flanks, and the variations in the angles of their surface slopes; studying the way their boulders had been assorted and related and brought to rest, and their correspondence in size with the cleavage joints of the cliffs from whence they were derived, cautious about making up my mind. But at last all doubt as to their formation vanished.

At half-past two o'clock of a moonlit morning in March, I was awakened by a tremendous earthquake, and though I had never before enjoyed a storm of this sort, the strange thrilling motion could not be mistaken, and I ran out of my cabin, both glad and frightened, shouting, "A noble earthquake! A noble earthquake!" feeling sure I was going to learn something. The shocks were so violent and varied, and succeeded one another so closely, that I had to balance myself carefully in walking as if on the deck of a ship among waves, and it seemed impossible that the high cliffs of the Valley could escape being shattered. In particular, I feared that the sheer-fronted Sentinel Rock, towering above my cabin, would be shaken down, and I took shelter back of a large yellow pine, hoping that it might protect me from at least the smaller outbounding boulders. For a minute or two the shocks became more and more violent—flashing horizontal thrusts mixed with a few twists and battering, explosive, upheaving jolts,—as if Nature were wrecking her Yosemite temple, and getting ready to build a still better one.

I was now convinced before a single boulder had fallen that earthquakes were the talus-makers and positive proof soon came. It was a calm moonlight night, and no sound was heard for the first minute or so, save low, muffled, underground, bubbling rumblings, and the whispering and rustling of the agitated trees, as if Nature were holding her breath. Then, suddenly, out of the strange silence and strange motion there came a tremendous roar. The Eagle Rock on the south wall, about a half a mile up the

Snow Banners

Valley, gave way and I saw it falling in thousands of the great boulders I had so long been studying, pouring to the Valley floor in a free curve luminous from friction, making a terribly sublime spectacle—an arc of glowing, passionate fire, fifteen hundred feet span, as true in form and as serene in beauty as a rainbow in the midst of the stupendous, roaring rock-storm. The sound was so tremendously deep and broad and earnest, the whole earth like a living creature seemed to have at last found a voice and to be calling to her sister planets. In trying to tell something of the size of this awful sound it seems to me that if all the thunder of all the storms I had ever heard were condensed into one roar it would not equal this rock-roar at the birth of a mountain talus. Think, then, of the roar that arose to heaven at the simultaneous birth of all the thousands of ancient cañon-taluses throughout the length and breadth of the Range!

The first severe shocks were soon over, and eager to examine the new-born talus I ran up the Valley in the moonlight and climbed upon it before the huge blocks, after their fiery flight, had come to complete rest. They were slowly settling into their places, chafing, grating against one another, groaning, and whispering; but no motion was visible except in a stream of small fragments pattering down the face of the cliff. A cloud of dust particles, lighted by the moon, floated out across the whole breadth of the Valley, forming a ceiling that lasted until after sunrise, and the air was filled with the odor of crushed Douglas spruces from a grove that had been mowed down and mashed like weeds.

After the ground began to calm I ran across the meadow to the river to see in what direction it was flowing and was glad to find that *down* the Valley was still down. Its waters were muddy from portions of its banks having given way, but it was flowing around its curves and over its ripples and shallows with ordinary tones and gestures. The mud would soon be cleared away and the raw slips on the banks would be the only visible record of the shaking it suffered.

The Upper Yosemite Fall, glowing white in the moonlight, seemed to know nothing of the earthquake, manifesting no change in form or voice, as far as I could see or hear.

After a second startling shock, about half-past three o'clock, the ground continued to tremble gently, and smooth, hollow rumbling sounds, not always distinguishable from the rounded, bumping, explosive tones of the falls, came from deep in the mountains in a northern direction.

The few Indians fled from their huts to the middle of the Valley, fearing that angry spirits were trying to kill them; and, as I afterward learned, most of the Yosemite tribe, who were spending the winter at their village on Bull Creek forty miles away, were so terrified that they ran into the river and washed themselves,—getting themselves clean enough to say their prayers, I suppose, or to die. I asked Dick, one of the Indians with whom I was acquainted, "What made the ground shake and jump so much?" He only shook his head and said, "No good. No good," and looked appealingly to me to give him hope that his life was to be spared.

In the morning I found the few white settlers assembled in front of the old Hutchings Hotel comparing notes and meditating flight to the lowlands, seemingly as sorely frightened as the Indians. Shortly after sunrise a low, blunt, muffled rumbling, like distant thunder, was followed by another series of shocks, which, though not nearly so severe as the first, made the cliffs and domes tremble like jelly, and the big pines and oaks thrill and swish and wave their branches with startling effect. Then the talkers were suddenly hushed, and the solemnity on their faces was sublime. One in particular of these winter neighbors, a somewhat speculative thinker with whom I had often conversed, was a firm believer in the cataclysmic origin of the Valley; and I now jokingly remarked that his wild tumble-down-and-engulfment hypothesis might soon be proved, since these underground rumblings and shakings might be the forerunners of another Yosemite-making cataclysm, which would perhaps double the depth of the Valley by swallowing the floor, leaving the ends of the roads and trails dangling three or four thousand feet in the air. Just then came the third series of shocks, and it was fine to see how awfully silent and solemn he became. His belief in the existence of a mysterious abyss, into which the suspended floor of the Valley and all the domes and battlements of the walls might at any moment go roaring down, mightily troubled him. To diminish his fears and laugh him into something like reasonable faith, I said, "Come, cheer up; smile a little and clap your hands, now that kind Mother Earth is trotting us on her knee to amuse us and make us good." But the well-meant joke seemed irreverent and utterly failed, as if only prayerful terror could rightly belong to the wild beauty-making business. Even after all the heavier shocks were over I could do nothing to reassure him. On the contrary, he handed me the keys of his little store to keep, saying that with a companion of like mind he was going to the lowlands to stay until the fate of poor, trembling Yosemite was settled. In vain I rallied them on their fears, calling attention to the strength of the granite walls of our Valley home, the very best and solidest masonry in the world, and less likely to collapse and sink than the sedimentary lowlands to which they were looking for safety; and saying that in any case they sometime would have to die, and so grand a burial was not to be slighted. But they were too seriously panic-stricken to get comfort from anything I could say.

During the third severe shock the trees were so violently shaken that the birds flew out with frightened cries. In particular, I noticed two robins flying in terror from a leafless oak, the branches of which swished and quivered as if struck by a heavy battering-ram. Exceedingly interesting were the flashing and quivering of the elastic needles of the pines in the sunlight and the waving up and down of the branches while the trunks stood rigid. There was no swaying, waving or swirling as in wind-storms, but quick, quivering jerks, and at times the heavy tasseled branches moved as if they had all been pressed down against the trunk and suddenly let go, to spring up and vibrate until they came to rest again. Only the owls seemed to be undisturbed. Before the rumbling echoes had died away a hollow-voiced owl began to hoot in philosophical tranquillity from near the edge of the new talus as if nothing extraordinary had occurred, although, perhaps, he was curious to know what all the noise was about. His "hoot-too-hoot-too-whoo" might have meant, "what's a' the steer, kimmer?"

It was long before the Valley found perfect rest. The rocks trembled more or less every day for over two months, and I kept a bucket of water on my table to learn what I could of the movements. The blunt thunder in the depths of the mountains was usually followed by sudden jarring, horizontal thrusts from the northward, often succeeded by twisting, upjolting movements. More than a month after the first great shock, when I was standing on a fallen tree up the Valley near Lamon's winter cabin, I heard a

Snow Banners

distinct bubbling thunder from the direction of Tenaya Cañon. Carlo, a large intelligent St. Bernard dog standing beside me seemed greatly astonished, and looked intently in that direction with mouth open and uttered a low *Wouf!* as if saying, "What's that?" He must have known that it was not thunder, though like it. The air was perfectly still, not the faintest breath of wind perceptible, and a fine, mellow, sunny hush pervaded everything, in the midst of which came that subterranean thunder. Then, while we gazed and listened, came the corresponding shocks, distinct as if some mighty hand had shaken the ground. After the sharp horizontal jars died away, they were followed by a gentle rocking and undulating of the ground so distinct that Carlo looked at the log on which he was standing to see who was shaking it. It was the season of flooded meadows and the pools about me, calm as sheets of glass, were suddenly thrown into low ruffling waves.

Judging by its effects, this Yosemite, or Inyo earthquake, as it is sometimes called, was gentle as compared with the one that gave rise to the grand talus system of the Range and did so much for the cañon scenery. Nature, usually so deliberate in her operations, then created, as we have seen, a new set of features, simply by giving the mountains a shake—changing not only the high peaks and cliffs, but the streams. As soon as these rock avalanches fell, the streams began to sing new songs; for in many places thousands of boulders were hurled into their channels, roughening and half-damming them, compelling the waters to surge and roar in rapids where before they glided smoothly. Some of the streams were completely dammed; driftwood, leaves, etc., gradually filling the interstices between the boulders, thus giving rise to lakes and level reaches; and these again, after being gradually filled in, were

[63]

changed to meadows, through which the streams are now silently meandering; while at the same time some of the taluses took the places of old meadows and groves. Thus rough places were made smooth, and smooth places rough. But, on the whole, by what at first sight seemed pure confounded confusion and ruin, the landscapes were enriched; for gradually every talus was covered with groves and gardens, and made a finely proportioned and ornamental base for the cliffs. In this work of beauty, every boulder is prepared and measured and put in its place more thoughtfully than are the stones of temples. If for a moment you are inclined to regard these taluses as mere draggled, chaotic dumps, climb to the top of one of them, and run down without any haggling, puttering hesitation, boldly jumping from boulder to boulder with even speed. You will then find your feet playing a tune, and quickly discover the music and poetry of these magnificent rock piles—a fine lesson; and all Nature's wildness tells the same story—the shocks and outbursts of earthquakes, volcanoes, geysers, roaring, thundering waves and floods, the silent uprush of sap in plants, storms of every sort—each and all are the orderly beauty-making love-beats of Nature's heart.

5

The Trees of the Valley

THE most influential of the Valley trees is the yellow pine (*Pinus ponderosa*). It attains its noblest dimensions on beds of water-washed, coarsely-stratified moraine material, between the talus slopes and meadows, dry on the surface, well-watered below and where not too closely assembled in groves the branches reach nearly to the ground, forming grand spires 200 to 220 feet in height. The largest that I have measured is standing alone almost opposite the Sentinel Rock, or a little to the westward of it. It is a little over eight feet in diameter and about 220 feet high. Climbing these grand trees, especially when they are waving and singing in worship in wind-storms, is a glorious experience. Ascending from the lowest branch to the topmost is like stepping up stairs through a blaze of white light, every needle thrilling and shining as if with religious ecstasy.

Unfortunately there are but few sugar pines in the Valley, though in the King's yosemite they are in glorious abundance. The incense cedar (*Libocedrus decurrens*) with cinnamon-colored bark and yellow-green foliage is one of the most interesting of the Yo-semite trees. Some of them are 150 feet high, from six to ten feet in diameter, and they are never out of sight as you saunter among the yellow pines. Their bright brown shafts and towers of flat, frondlike branches make a striking feature of the landscapes throughout all the seasons. In midwinter, when most of the other trees are asleep, this cedar puts forth its flowers in millions,—the pistillate pale green and inconspicuous, but the staminate bright yellow, tingeing all the branches and making the trees as they stand in the snow look like gigantic goldenrods. The branches, outspread in flat plumes and, beautifully fronded, sweep gracefully downward and outward, except those near the top, which aspire; the lowest, especially in youth and middle age, droop to the ground, overlapping one another, shedding off rain and snow like shingles, and making fine tents for birds and campers. This tree frequently lives more than a thousand years and is well worthy its place beside the great pines and the Douglas spruce.

The two largest specimens I know of the Douglas spruce, about eight feet in diameter, are growing at the foot of the Liberty Cap near the Nevada Fall, and on the terminal moraine of the small residual glacier that lingered in the shady Illilouette Cañon.

After the conifers, the most important of the Yosemite trees are the oaks, two species; the California live-oak (*Quercus agrifolia*), with black trunks, reaching a thickness of from four to nearly seven feet, wide spreading branches and bright deeply-scalloped leaves. It occupies the greater part of the broad sandy flats of the upper end of the Valley, and is the species that yields the acorns so highly prized by the Indians and woodpeckers.

The other species is the mountain live-oak, or goldcup oak (*Quercus chrysolepis*), a sturdy mountaineer of a tree, growing mostly on the earthquake taluses and benches of the sunny north wall of the Valley. In tough, unwedgeable, knotty strength, it is the oak of oaks, a magnificent tree.

The largest and most picturesque specimen in the Valley is near the foot of the Tenaya Fall, a romantic spot seldom seen on account of the rough trouble of getting to it. It is planted on three huge boulders and yet manages to draw sufficient moisture and food from this craggy soil to maintain itself in good health. It is twenty feet in circumference, measured above a large branch between three and four feet in diameter that has been broken off. The main knotty trunk seems to be made up of craggy granite boulders like those on which it stands, being about the same color as the mossy, lichened boulders and about as rough. Two moss-lined caves near the ground open back into the trunk, one on the north side, the other on the west, forming picturesque, romantic seats. The largest of the main branches is eighteen feet and nine inches in circumference, and some of the long pendulous branchlets droop over the stream at the foot of the fall where it is gray with spray. The leaves are glossy yellow-green, ever in motion from the wind from the fall. It is a fine place to dream in, with falls, cascades, cool rocks lined with hypnum three inches thick; shaded with maple, dogwood, alder, willow; grand clumps of lady-ferns where no hand may touch them; light filtering through translucent leaves; oaks fifty feet high; lilies eight feet high in a filled lake basin near by, and the finest libocedrus groves and tallest ferns and goldenrods.

In the main river cañon below the Vernal Fall and on the shady south side of the Valley there are a few groves of the silver fir (*Abies concolor*), and superb forests of the magnificent species around the rim of the Valley.

On the tops of the domes is found the sturdy, storm-enduring red cedar (*Juniperus occidentalis*). It never makes anything like a forest here, but stands out separate and independent in the wind, clinging by slight joints to the rock, with scarce a handful of soil in sight of it, seeming to depend chiefly on snow and air for nourishment, and yet it has maintained tough health on this diet for two thousand years or more. The largest hereabouts are from five to six feet in diameter and fifty feet in height.

The principal river-side trees are poplar, alder, willow, broad-leaved maple, and Nuttall's flowering dogwood. The poplar (*Populus trichocarpa*), often called balm-of-Gilead from the gum on its buds, is a tall tree, towering above its companions and gracefully embowering the banks of the river. Its abundant foliage turns bright yellow in the fall, and the Indian-summer sunshine sifts through it in delightful tones over the slow-gliding waters when they are at their lowest ebb.

Some of the involucres of the flowering dogwood measure six to eight inches in diameter, and the whole tree when in flower looks as if covered with snow. In the spring when the streams are in flood it is the whitest of trees. In Indian summer the leaves become bright crimson, making a still grander show than the flowers.

The broad-leaved maple and mountain maple are found mostly in the cool cañons at the head of the Valley, spreading their branches in beautiful arches over the foaming streams.

Scattered here and there are a few other trees, mostly small— the mountain mahogany, cherry, chestnut-oak, and laurel. The California nutmeg (*Torreya californica*), a handsome evergreen, belonging to the yew family, forms small groves near the cascades a mile or two below the foot of the Valley.

6

The Forest Trees in General

FOR the use of the ever-increasing number of Yosemite visitors who make extensive excursions into the mountains beyond the Valley, a sketch of the forest trees in general will probably be found useful. The different species are arranged in zones and sections, which brings the forest as a whole within the comprehension of every observer. These species are always found as controlled by the climates of different elevations, by soil and by the comparative strength of each species in taking and holding possession of the ground; and so appreciable are these relations the traveler need never be at a loss in determining within a few hundred feet his elevation above sea level by the trees alone; for, notwithstanding some of the species range upward for several thousand feet and all pass one another more or less, yet even those species possessing the greatest vertical range are available in measuring the elevation; inasmuch as they take on new forms corresponding with variations in altitude. Entering the lower fringe of the forest composed of Douglas oaks and Sabine pines, the trees grow so far apart that not one-twentieth of the surface of the ground is in shade at noon. After advancing fifteen or twenty miles towards Yosemite and making an ascent of from two to three thousand feet you reach the lower margin of the main pine belt, composed of great sugar pine, yellow pine, incense cedar and sequoia. Next you come to the magnificent silver-fir belt and lastly to the upper pine belt, which sweeps up to the feet of the summit peaks in a dwarfed fringe, to a height

The Yosemite

of from ten to twelve thousand feet. That this general order of distribution depends on climate as affected by height above the sea, is seen at once, but there are other harmonies that become manifest only after observation and study. One of the most interesting of these is the arrangement of the forest in long curving bands, braided together into lace-like patterns in some places and outspread in charming variety. The key to these striking arrangements is the system of ancient glaciers; where they flowed the trees followed, tracing their courses along the sides of cañons, over ridges, and high plateaus. The cedar of Lebanon, said Sir Joseph Hooker, occurs upon one of the moraines of an ancient glacier. All the forests of the Sierra are growing upon moraines, but moraines vanish like the glaciers that make them. Every storm that falls upon them wastes them, carrying away their decaying, disintegrating material into new formations, until they are no longer recognizable without tracing their transitional forms down the Range from those still in process of formation in some places through those that are more and more ancient and more obscured by vegetation and all kinds of post-glacial weathering. It appears, therefore, that the Sierra forests indicate the extent and positions of ancient moraines as well as they do belts of climate.

One will have no difficulty in knowing the Nut Pine (*Pinus Sabiniana*), for it is the first conifer met in ascending the Range from the west, springing up here and there among Douglas oaks and thickets of ceanothus and manzanita; its extreme upper limit being about 4000 feet above the sea, its lower about from 500 to 800 feet. It is remarkable for its loose, airy, wide-branching habit, and thin gray foliage. Full-grown specimens are from forty to fifty feet in height and from two to three feet in diameter. The trunk usually divides into three or four main branches about fifteen or twenty feet from the ground that, after bearing away from one another, shoot straight up and form separate summits. Their slender, grayish needles are from eight to twelve inches long, and inclined to droop, contrasting with the rigid, dark-colored trunk and branches. No other tree of my acquaintance so substantial in its body has foliage so thin and pervious to the light. The cones are from five to eight inches long and about as large in thickness; rich chocolate-brown in color and protected by strong, down-curving hooks which terminate the scales. Nevertheless the little Douglas squirrel can open them. Indians climb the trees like bears and beat off the cones or recklessly cut off the more fruitful branches with hatchets, while the squaws gather and roast them until the scales open sufficiently to allow the hard-shell seeds to be beaten out. The curious little *Pinus attenuata* is found at an elevation of from 1500 to 3000 feet, growing in close groves and belts. It is exceedingly slender and graceful, although trees that chance to stand alone send out very long, curved branches, making a striking contrast to the ordinary grove form. The foliage is of the same peculiar gray-green color as that of the nut pine, and is worn about as loosely, so that the body of the tree is scarcely obscured by it. At the age of seven or eight years it begins to bear cones in whorls on the main axis, and as they never fall off, the trunk is soon picturesquely dotted with them. Branches also soon become fruitful. The average size of the tree is about thirty or forty feet in height and twelve to fourteen inches in diameter. The cones are about four inches long, and covered with a sort of varnish and gum, rendering them impervious to moisture.

No observer can fail to notice the admirable adaptation of this curious pine to the fire-swept regions where alone it is found. After a running fire has scorched and killed it the cones open and the ground beneath it is then sown broadcast with all the seeds ripened during its whole life. Then up spring a crowd of bright, hopeful seedlings, giving beauty for ashes in lavish abundance.

THE SUGAR PINE, KING OF PINE TREES

Of all the world's eighty or ninety species of pine trees, the Sugar Pine (*Pinus Lambertiana*) is king, surpassing all others, not merely in size but in lordly beauty and majesty. In the Yosemite region it grows at an elevation of from 3000 to 7000 feet above the sea and attains most perfect development at a height of about 5000 feet. The largest specimens are commonly about 220 feet high and from six to eight feet in diameter four feet from the ground, though some grand old patriarch may be met here and there that has enjoyed six or eight centuries of storms and attained a thickness of ten or even twelve feet, still sweet and fresh in every fiber. The trunk is a re-markably smooth, round, delicately-tapered shaft, straight and regular as if turned in a lathe, mostly without limbs, purplish brown in color and usually enlivened with tufts of a yellow lichen. Toward the head of this magnificent column long branches sweep gracefully outward and downward, sometimes forming a palm-like crown, but far more impressive than any palm crown I ever beheld. The needles are about three inches long in fascicles of five, and arranged in rather close tassels at the ends of slender branchlets that clothe the long outsweeping limbs. How well they sing in the wind, and how strikingly harmonious an effect is made by the long cylindrical cones, depending loosely from the ends of the long branches! The cones are about fifteen to eighteen inches long, and three in diameter; green, shaded with dark purple on their sunward sides. They are ripe in September and October of the second year from the flower. Then the flat, thin scales open and the seeds take wing, but the empty cones become still more beautiful and effective as decorations, for their diameter is nearly doubled by the spreading of the scales, and their color changes to yellowish brown while they remain, swinging on the tree all the following winter and summer, and continue effectively beautiful even on the ground many years after they fall. The wood is deliciously fragrant, fine in grain and texture and creamy yellow, as if formed of condensed sunbeams. The sugar from which the common name is derived is, I think, the best of sweets. It exudes from the heart-wood where wounds have been made by forest fires or the ax, and forms irregular, crisp, candy-like kernels of considerable size, something like clusters of resin beads. When fresh it is white, but because most of the wounds on which it is found have been made by fire the sap is stained and the hardened sugar becomes brown. Indians are fond of it, but on account of its laxative properties only small quantities may be eaten. No tree lover will ever forget his first meeting with the sugar pine. In most pine trees there is the sameness of expression which to most people is apt to become monotonous, for the typical spiral form of conifers, however beautiful, affords little scope for appreciable individual character. The sugar pine is as free from conventionalities as the most picturesque oaks. No two are alike, and though they toss out their immense arms in what might seem extravagant gestures they never lose their expression of serene majesty. They are the priests of pines and seem ever to be addressing the surrounding forest. The yellow pine is found growing with them on warm hillsides, and the silver fir on cool northern slopes; but, noble as these are, the sugar pine is easily king, and spreads his arms above them in blessing while they rock and wave in sign of recognition. The main branches are sometimes forty feet long, yet persistently simple, seldom dividing at all, excepting near the end; but anything like a bare cable appearance is prevented by the small, tasseled branchlets that extend all around them; and when these superb limbs sweep out symmetrically on all sides, a crown sixty or seventy feet wide is formed, which, gracefully poised on the summit of the noble shaft, is a glorious object. Commonly, however, there is a preponderance of limbs toward the east, away from the direction of the prevailing winds.

Although so unconventional when full-grown, the sugar pine is a remarkably proper tree in youth—a strict follower of coniferous fashions—slim, erect, with leafy branches kept exactly in place, each tapering in outline and terminating in a spiry point. The successive forms between the cautious neatness of youth and the bold freedom of maturity offer a delightful study. At the age of fifty or sixty years, the shy, fashionable form begins to be broken up. Specialized branches push out and bend with the great cones, giving individual character, that becomes more marked from year to year. Its most constant companion is the yellow pine. The Douglas spruce, libocedrus, sequoia, and the silver fir are also more or less associated with it; but on many deep-soiled mountain-sides, at an elevation of about 5000 feet above the sea, it forms the bulk of the forest, filling every swell and hollow and down-plunging ravine. The majestic crowns, approaching each other in bold curves, make a glorious canopy through which the tempered sunbeams pour, silvering the needles, and gilding the massive boles and the flowery, park-like ground into a scene of enchantment.

The Forest Trees in General

On the most sunny slopes the white-flowered, fragrant cha-
maebatia is spread like a carpet, brightened during early summer
with the crimson sarcodes, the wild rose, and innumerable violets
and gilias. Not even in the shadiest nooks will you find any rank,
untidy weeds or unwholesome darkness. In the north sides of
ridges the boles are more slender, and the ground is mostly occupied by an underbrush of hazel, ceanothus, and flowering dogwood, but not so densely as to prevent the traveler from sauntering
where he will; while the crowning branches are never impenetrable
to the rays of the sun, and never so interblended as to lose their
individuality.

THE YELLOW OR SILVER PINE

The Silver Pine (*Pinus ponderosa*), or Yellow Pine, as it is commonly called, ranks second among the pines of the Sierra as a
lumber tree, and almost rivals the sugar pine in stature and noble-
ness of port. Because of its superior powers of enduring variations
of climate and soil, it has a more extensive range than any other
conifer growing on the Sierra. On the western slope it is first met
at an elevation of about 2000 feet, and extends nearly to the upper
limit of the timber-line. Thence, crossing the range by the lowest
passes, it descends to the eastern base, and pushes out for a considerable distance into the hot, volcanic plains, growing bravely upon
well-watered moraines, gravelly lake basins, climbing old volcanoes and dropping ripe cones among ashes and cinders.

The average size of full-grown trees on the western slope,
where it is associated with the sugar pine, is a little less than 200
feet in height and from five to six feet in diameter, though specimens considerably larger may easily be found. Where there is

plenty of free sunshine and other conditions are favorable, it presents a striking contrast in form to the sugar pine, being a symmetrical spire, formed of a straight round trunk, clad with innumerable branches that are divided over and over again. Unlike the Yosemite form about one-half of the trunk is commonly branchless, but where it grows at all close three-fourths or more is naked, presenting then a more slender and elegant shaft than any other tree in the woods. The bark is mostly arranged in massive plates, some of them measuring four or five feet in length by eighteen inches in width, with a thickness of three or four inches, forming a quite marked and distinguishing feature. The needles are of a fine, warm, yellow-green color, six to eight inches long, firm and elastic, and crowded in handsome, radiant tassels on the upturning ends of the branches. The cones are about three or four inches long, and two and a half wide, growing in close, sessile clusters among the leaves.

The species attains its noblest form in filled-up lake basins, especially in those of the older yosemites, and as we have seen, so prominent a part does it form of their groves that it may well be called the Yosemite Pine.

The Jeffrey variety attains its finest development in the northern portion of the Range, in the wide basins of the McCloud and Pitt Rivers, where it forms magnificent forests scarcely invaded by any other tree. It differs from the ordinary form in size, being only about half as tall, in its redder and more closely-furrowed bark, grayish-green foliage, less divided branches, and much larger cones; but intermediate forms come in which make a clear separation impossible, although some botanists regard it as a distinct species. It is this variety of ponderosa that climbs storm-swept ridges alone, and wanders out among the volcanoes of the Great Basin. Whether exposed to extremes of heat or cold, it is dwarfed like many other trees, and becomes all knots and angles, wholly unlike the majestic forms we have been sketching. Old specimens, bearing cones about as big as pineapples, may sometimes be found clinging to rifted rocks at an elevation of 7000 or 8000 feet, whose highest branches scarce reach above one's shoulders.

I have often feasted on the beauty of these noble trees when they were towering in all their winter grandeur, laden with snow—one mass of bloom; in summer, too, when the brown, staminate clusters hang thick among the shimmering needles, and the big purple burrs are ripening in the mellow light; but it is during cloudless wind-storms that these colossal pines are most impressively beautiful. Then they bow like willows, their leaves streaming forward all in one direction, and, when the sun shines upon them at the required angle, entire groves glow as if every leaf were burnished silver. The fall of tropic light on the crown of a palm is a truly glorious spectacle, the fervid sun-flood breaking upon the glossy leaves in long lance-rays, like mountain water among boulders at the foot of an enthusiastic cataract. But to me there is something more impressive in the fall of light upon these noble, silver pine pillars: it is beaten to the finest dust and shed off in myriads of minute sparkles that seem to radiate from the very heart of the tree, as if like rain, falling upon fertile soil, it had been absorbed to reappear in flowers of light. This species also gives forth the finest wind music. After listening to it in all kinds of winds, night and day, season after season, I think I could approximate to my position on the mountain by this pine music alone. If you would catch the tone of separate needles climb a tree in breezy weather. Every

The Yosemite

needle is carefully tempered and gives forth no uncertain sound, each standing out with no interference excepting during heavy gales; then you may detect the click of one needle upon another, readily distinguishable from the free wind-like hum.

When a sugar pine and one of this species equal in size are observed together, the latter is seen to be more simple in manners, more lively and graceful, and its beauty is of a kind more easily appreciated; on the other hand it is less dignified and original in demeanor. The yellow pine seems ever eager to shoot aloft, higher and higher. Even while it is drowsing in autumn sun-gold you may still detect a skyward aspiration, but the sugar pine seems too unconsciously noble and too complete in every way to leave room for even a heavenward care.

THE DOUGLAS SPRUCE

The Douglas Spruce (*Pseudotsuga Douglasii*) is one of the largest and longest-lived of the giants that flourish throughout the main pine belt, often attaining a height of nearly 200 feet, and a diameter of six or seven feet. Where the growth is not too close, the stout, spreading branches, covering more than half of the trunk, are hung with innumerable slender, drooping sprays, handsomely feathered with the short leaves which radiate at right angles all around them. This vigorous tree is ever beautiful, welcoming the mountain winds and the snow as well as the mellow summer light; and it maintains its youthful freshness undiminished from century to century through a thousand storms. It makes its finest appearance during the months of June and July, when the brown buds at the ends of the sprays swell and open, revealing the young leaves,

[78]

which at first are bright yellow, making the tree appear as if covered with gay blossoms; while the pendulous bracted cones, three or four inches long, with their shell-like scales, are a constant adornment.

The young trees usually are assembled in family groups, each sapling exquisitely symmetrical. The primary branches are whorled regularly around the axis, generally in fives, while each is draped with long, feathery sprays that descend in lines as free and as finely drawn as those of falling water.

In Oregon and Washington it forms immense forests, growing tall and mast-like to a height of 300 feet, and is greatly prized as a lumber tree. Here it is scattered among other trees, or forms small groves, seldom ascending higher than 5500 feet, and never making what would be called a forest. It is not particular in its choice of soil: wet or dry, smooth or rocky, it makes out to live well on them all. Two of the largest specimens, as we have seen, are in Yosemite; one of these, more than eight feet in diameter, is growing on a moraine; the other, nearly as large, on angular blocks of granite. No other tree in the Sierra seems so much at home on earthquake taluses and many of these huge boulder-slopes are almost exclusively occupied by it.

THE INCENSE CEDAR

Incense Cedar (*Libocedrus decurrens*), already noticed among the Yosemite trees, is quite generally distributed throughout the pine belt without exclusively occupying any considerable area, or even making extensive groves. On the warmer mountain slopes it ascends to about 5000 feet, and reaches the climate most congenial

to it at a height of about 4000 feet, growing vigorously at this elevation in all kinds of soil and, in particular, it is capable of enduring more moisture about its roots than any of its companions
excepting only the sequoia.

Casting your eye over the general forest from some ridge-top
you can identify it by the color alone of its spiry summits, a warm
yellow-green. In its youth up to the age of seventy or eighty years,
none of its companions forms so strictly tapered a cone from top to
bottom. As it becomes older it oftentimes grows strikingly irregular
and picturesque. Large branches push out at right angles to the
trunk, forming stubborn elbows and shoot up parallel with the axis.
Very old trees are usually dead at the top. The flat fragrant plumes
are exceedingly beautiful: no waving fern-frond is finer in form and
texture. In its prime the whole tree is thatched with them, but if
you would see the libocedrus in all its glory you must go to the
woods in midwinter when it is laden with myriads of yellow flowers
about the size of wheat grains, forming a noble illustration of Nature's immortal virility and vigor. The mature cones, about three-
fourths of an inch long, born on the ends of the plumy branchlets,
serve to enrich still more the surpassing beauty of this winter-
blooming tree-goldenrod.

THE SILVER FIRS

We come now to the most regularly planted and most clearly defined of the main forest belts, composed almost exclusively of two
Silver Firs—*Abies concolor* and *Abies magnifica*—extending with
but little interruption 450 miles at an elevation of from 5000 to
9000 feet above the sea. In its youth A. *concolor* is a charmingly

The Forest Trees in General

symmetrical tree with its flat plumy branches arranged in regular whorls around the whitish-gray axis which terminates in a stout, hopeful shoot, pointing straight to the zenith, like an admonishing finger. The leaves are arranged in two horizontal rows along branchlets that commonly are less than eight years old, forming handsome plumes, pinnated like the fronds of ferns. The cones are grayish-green when ripe, cylindrical, from three to four inches long, and one and a half to two inches wide, and stand upright on the upper horizontal branches. Full-grown trees in favorable situations are usually about 200 feet high and five or six feet in diameter. As old age creeps on, the rough bark becomes rougher and grayer, the branches lose their exact regularity of form, many that are snow-bent are broken off and the axis often becomes double or otherwise irregular from accidents to the terminal bud or shoot. Nevertheless, throughout all the vicissitudes of its three or four centuries of life, come what may, the noble grandeur of this species, however obscured, is never lost.

The magnificent Silver Fir, or California Red Fir (*Abies magnifica*) is the most symmetrical of all the Sierra giants, far surpassing its companion species in this respect and easily distinguished from it by the purplish-red bark, which is also more closely furrowed than that of the white, and by its larger cones, its more regularly whorled and fronded branches, and its shorter leaves, which grow all around the branches and point upward instead of being arranged in two horizontal rows. The branches are mostly whorled in fives, and stand out from the straight, red-purple bole in level, or in old trees in drooping collars, every branch regularly pinnated like fern-fronds, making broad plumes, singularly rich and sumptuous-looking. The flowers are in their prime about the middle of June; the male red, growing on the underside of the branches in crowded profusion, giving a very rich color to all the trees; the female greenish-yellow, tinged with pink, standing erect on the upper side of the topmost branches, while the tufts of young leaves, about as brightly colored as those of the Douglas spruce, make another grand show. The cones mature in a single season from the flowers. When mature they are about six to eight inches long, three or four in diameter, covered with a fine gray down and streaked and beaded with transparent balsam, very rich and precious-looking, and stand erect like casks on the topmost branches. The inside of the cone is, if possible, still more beautiful. The scales and bracts are tinged with red and the seed-wings are purple with bright iridescence. Both of the silver firs live between two and three centuries when the conditions about them are at all favorable. Some venerable patriarch may be seen heavily storm-marked, towering in severe majesty above the rising generation, with a protecting grove of hopeful saplings pressing close around his feet, each dressed with such loving care that not a leaf seems wanting. Other groups are made up of trees near the prime of life, nicely arranged as if Nature had culled them with discrimination from all the rest of the woods. It is from this tree, called Red Fir by the lumbermen, that mountaineers cut boughs to sleep on when they are so fortunate as to be within its limit. Two or three rows of the sumptuous plushy-fronded branches, overlapping along the middle, and a crescent of smaller plumes mixed to one's taste with ferns and flowers for a pillow, form the very best bed imaginable. The essence of the pressed leaves seems to fill every pore of one's body. Falling water makes a soothing hush, while the spaces between the grand spires afford noble openings through which to gaze dreamily into

The Forest Trees in General

the starry sky. The fir woods are fine sauntering-grounds at almost any time of the year, but finest in autumn when the noble trees are hushed in the hazy light and drip with balsam; and the flying, whirling seeds, escaping from the ripe cones, mottle the air like flocks of butterflies. Even in the richest part of these unrivaled forests where so many noble trees challenge admiration we linger fondly among the colossal firs and extol their beauty again and again, as if no other tree in the world could henceforth claim our love. It is in these woods the great granite domes arise that are so striking and characteristic a feature of the Sierra. Here, too, we find the best of the garden-meadows full of lilies. A dry spot a little way back from the margin of a silver fir lily-garden makes a glorious camp-ground, especially where the slope is toward the east with a view of the distant peaks along the summit of the Range. The tall lilies are brought forward most impressively like visitors by the light of your camp-fire and the nearest of the trees with their whorled branches tower above you like larger lilies and the sky seen through the garden-opening seems one vast meadow of white lily stars.

THE TWO-LEAVED PINE

The Two-Leaved Pine (*Pinus contorta*, var. *Murrayana*), above the Silver Fir zone, forms the bulk of the alpine forests up to a height of from 8000 to 9500 feet above the sea, growing in beautiful order on moraines scarcely changed as yet by post-glacial weathering. Compared with the giants of the lower regions this is a small tree, seldom exceeding a height of eighty or ninety feet. The largest I ever measured was ninety feet high and a little over six feet in diameter. The average height of mature trees throughout the entire belt is probably not far from fifty or sixty feet with a diameter of two feet. It is a well-proportioned, rather handsome tree with grayish-brown bark and crooked, much-divided branches which cover the greater part of the trunk, but not so densely as to prevent it being seen. The lower limbs, like those of most other conifers that grow in snowy regions, curve downward, gradually take a horizontal position about half-way up the trunk, then aspire more and more toward the summit. The short, rigid needles in fascicles of two are arranged in comparatively long cylindrical tassels at the ends of the tough up-curving branches. The cones are about two inches long, growing in clusters among the needles without any striking effect except while very young, when the flowers are of a vivid crimson color and the whole tree appears to be dotted with brilliant flowers. The staminate flowers are still more showy on account of their great abundance, often giving a reddish-yellow tinge to the whole mass of foliage and filling the air with pollen. No other pine on the Range is so regularly planted as this one, covering moraines that extend along the sides of the high rocky valleys for miles without interruption. The thin bark is streaked and sprinkled with resin as though it had been showered upon the forest like rain.

Therefore this tree more than any other is subject to destruction by fire. During strong winds extensive forests are destroyed, the flames leaping from tree to tree in continuous belts that go surging and racing onward above the bending wood like prairie-grass fires. During the calm season of Indian summer the fire creeps quietly along the ground, feeding on the needles and cones; arriving at the foot of a tree, the resiny bark is ignited and the heated air ascends in a swift current, increasing in velocity and dragging the flames upward. Then the leaves catch, forming an immense column of fire, beautifully spired on the edges and tinted a rose-purple hue. It rushes aloft thirty or forty feet above the top of the tree, forming a grand spectacle, especially at night. It lasts, however, only a few seconds, vanishing with magical rapidity, to be succeeded by others along the fire-line at irregular intervals, tree after tree, upflashing and darting, leaving the trunks and branches scarcely scarred. The heat, however, is sufficient to kill the tree and in a few years the bark shrivels and falls off. Forests miles in extent are thus killed and left standing, with the branches on, but peeled and rigid, appearing gray in the distance like misty clouds. Later the branches drop off, leaving a forest of bleached spars. At length the roots decay and the forlorn gray trunks are blown down during some storm and piled one upon another, encumbering the ground until, dry and seasoned, they are consumed by another fire and leave the ground ready for a fresh crop.

In sheltered lake-hollows, on beds of alluvium, this pine varies so far from the common form that frequently it could be taken for a distinct species, growing in damp sods like grasses from forty to eighty feet high, bending all together to the breeze and whirling in eddying gusts more lively than any other tree in the woods. I frequently found specimens fifty feet high less than five inches in diameter. Being so slender and at the same time clad with leafy boughs, it is often bent and weighed down to the ground when laden with soft snow; thus forming fine ornamental arches, many of them to last until the melting of the snow in the spring.

THE MOUNTAIN PINE

The Mountain Pine (*Pinus monticola*) is the noblest tree of the alpine zone—hardy and long-lived, towering grandly above its companions and becoming stronger and more imposing just where other species begin to crouch and disappear. At its best it is usually about ninety feet high and five or six feet in diameter, though you may find specimens here and there considerably larger than this. It is as massive and suggestive of enduring strength as an oak. About two-thirds of the trunk is commonly free of limbs, but close, fringy tufts of spray occur nearly all the way down to the ground. On trees that occupy exposed situations near its upper limit the bark is deep reddish-brown and rather deeply furrowed, the main furrows running nearly parallel to each other and connected on the old trees by conspicuous cross-furrows. The cones are from four to eight inches long, smooth, slender, cylindrical and somewhat curved. They grow in clusters of from three to six or seven and become pendulous as they increase in weight. This species is nearly related to the sugar pine and, though not half so tall, it suggests its noble relative in the way that it extends its long branches in general habit. It is first met on the upper margin of the silver fir zone, singly, in what appears as chance situations without making much impression on the general forest. Continuing up through the forests of the two-leaved pine it begins to show its distinguishing characteristic in the most marked way at an elevation of about 10,000 feet, extending its tough, rather slender arms in the frosty air, welcoming the storms and feeding on them and reaching sometimes to the grand old age of 1000 years.

THE WESTERN JUNIPER

The Juniper or Red Cedar (*Juniperus occidentalis*) is preëminently a rock tree, occupying the baldest domes and pavements in the upper silver fir and alpine zones, at a height of from 7000 to 9500 feet. In such situations, rooted in narrow cracks or fissures, where there is scarcely a handful of soil, it is frequently over eight feet in diameter and not much more in height. The tops of old trees are almost always dead, and large stubborn-looking limbs push out horizontally, most of them broken and dead at the end, but densely covered, and imbedded here and there with tufts or mounds of gray-green scalelike foliage. Some trees are mere storm-beaten stumps about as broad as long, decorated with a few leafy sprays, reminding one of the crumbling towers of old castles scantily draped with ivy. Its homes on bare, barren dome and ridge-top seem to have been chosen for safety against fire, for, on isolated mounds of sand and gravel free from grass and bushes on which fire could feed, it is often found growing tall and unscathed to a height of forty to sixty feet, with scarce a trace of the rocky angularity and broken limbs so characteristic a feature throughout the greater part of its range. It never makes anything like a forest; seldom even a grove. Usually it stands out separate and independent, clinging by slight joints to the rocks, living chiefly on snow and thin air and maintaining sound health on this diet for 2000 years or more. Every feature or every gesture it makes expresses steadfast, dogged endurance. The bark is of a bright cinnamon color and is handsomely braided and reticulated on thrifty trees, flaking off in thin, shining ribbons that are sometimes used by the Indians for tent matting. Its fine color and picturesqueness are appreciated by artists, but to me the juniper seems a singularly strange and taciturn tree. I have spent many a day and night in its company and always have found it silent and rigid. It seems to be a survivor of some ancient race, wholly unacquainted with its neighbors. Its broad stumpiness, of course, makes wind-waving or even shaking

[87]

out of the question, but it is not this rocky rigidity that constitutes its silence. In calm, sun-days the sugar pine preaches like an enthusiastic apostle without moving a leaf. On level rocks the juniper dies standing and wastes insensibly out of existence like granite, the wind exerting about as little control over it, alive or dead, as it does over a glacier boulder.

I have spent a good deal of time trying to determine the age of these wonderful trees, but as all of the very old ones are honeycombed with dry rot I never was able to get a complete count of the largest. Some are undoubtedly more than 2000 years old, for though on deep moraine soil they grow about as fast as some of the pines, on bare pavements and smoothly glaciated, overswept ridges in the dome region they grow very slowly. One on the Starr King Ridge only two feet eleven inches in diameter was 1140 years old forty years ago. Another on the same ridge, only one foot seven and a half inches in diameter, had reached the age of 834 years. The first fifteen inches from the bark of a medium-size tree six feet in diameter, on the north Tenaya pavement, had 859 layers of wood. Beyond this the count was stopped by dry rot and scars. The largest I examined was thirty-three feet in girth, or nearly ten feet in diameter and, although I have failed to get anything like a complete count, I learned enough from this and many other specimens to convince me that most of the trees eight or ten feet thick, standing on pavements, are more than twenty centuries old rather than less. Barring accidents, for all I can see they would live forever; even when overthrown by avalanches, they refuse to lie at rest, lean stubbornly on their big branches as if anxious to rise, and while a single root holds to the rock, put forth fresh leaves with a grim, never-say-die expression.

[88]

The Forest Trees in General

THE MOUNTAIN HEMLOCK

As the juniper is the most stubborn and unshakeable of trees in the Yosemite region, the Mountain Hemlock (*Tsuga Mertensiana*) is the most graceful and pliant and sensitive. Until it reaches a height of fifty or sixty feet it is sumptuously clothed down to the ground with drooping branches, which are divided again and again into delicate waving sprays, grouped and arranged in ways that are indescribably beautiful, and profusely adorned with small brown cones. The flowers also are peculiarly beautiful and effective; the female dark rich purple, the male blue, of so fine and pure a tone that the best azure of the mountain sky seems to be condensed in them. Though apparently the most delicate and feminine of all the mountain trees, it grows best where the snow lies deepest, at a height of from 9000 to 9500 feet, in hollows on the northern slopes of mountains and ridges. But under all circumstances, sheltered from heavy winds or in bleak exposure to them, well fed or starved, even at its highest limit, 10,500 feet above the sea, on exposed ridge-tops where it has to crouch and huddle close in low thickets, it still contrives to put forth its sprays and branches in forms of invincible beauty, while on moist, well-drained moraines it displays a perfectly tropical luxuriance of foliage, flowers and fruit. The snow of the first winter storm is frequently soft, and lodges in the dense leafy branches, weighing them down against the trunk, and the slender, drooping axis, bending lower and lower as the load increases, at length reaches the ground, forming an ornamental arch. Then, as storm succeeds storm and snow is heaped on snow, the whole tree is at last buried, not again to see the light of day or move leaf or limb until set free by the spring thaws in June or July.

The Yosemite

Not only the young saplings are thus carefully covered and put to sleep in the whitest of white beds for five or six months of the year, but trees thirty feet high or more. From April to May, when the snow by repeated thawing and freezing is firmly compacted, you may ride over the prostrate groves without seeing a single branch or leaf of them. No other of our alpine conifers so finely veils its strength; poised in thin, white sunshine, clad with branches from head to foot, it towers in unassuming majesty, drooping as if unaffected with the aspiring tendencies of its race, loving the ground, conscious of heaven and joyously receptive of its blessings, reaching out its branches like sensitive tentacles, feeling the light and reveling in it. The largest specimen I ever found was nineteen feet seven inches in circumference. It was growing on the edge of Lake Hollow, north of Mount Hoffman, at an elevation of 9250 feet above the level of the sea, and was probably about a hundred feet in height. Fine groves of mature trees, ninety to a hundred feet in height, are growing near the base of Mount Conness. It is widely distributed from near the south extremity of the high Sierra northward along the Cascade Mountains of Oregon and Washington and the coast ranges of British Columbia to Alaska, where it was first discovered in 1827. Its northernmost limit, so far as I have observed, is in the icy fiords of Prince William Sound in latitude 61°, where it forms pure forests at the level of the sea, growing tall and majestic on the banks of glaciers. There, as in the Yosemite region, it is ineffably beautiful, the very loveliest of all the American conifers.

The Forest Trees in General

THE WHITE-BARK PINE

The Dwarf Pine, or White-Bark Pine (*Pinus albicaulis*), forms the extreme edge of the timberline throughout nearly the whole extent of the Range on both flanks. It is first met growing with the two-leaved pine on the upper margin of the alpine belt, as an erect tree from fifteen to thirty feet high and from one to two feet in diameter; thence it goes straggling up the flanks of the summit peaks, upon moraines or crumbling ledges, wherever it can get a foothold, to an elevation of from 10,000 to 12,000 feet, where it dwarfs to a mass of crumpled branches, covered with slender shoots, each tipped with a short, close-packed, leaf tassel. The bark is smooth and purplish, in some places almost white. The flowers are bright scarlet and rose-purple, giving a very flowery appearance little looked for in such a tree. The cones are about three inches long, an inch and a half in diameter, grow in rigid clusters, and are dark chocolate in color while young, and bear beautiful pearly-white seeds about the size of peas, most of which are eaten by chipmunks and the Clarke's crows. Pines are commonly regarded as sky-loving trees that must necessarily aspire or die. This species forms a marked exception, crouching and creeping in compliance with the most rigorous demands of climate; yet enduring bravely to a more advanced age than many of its lofty relatives in the sun-lands far below it. Seen from a distance it would never be taken for a tree of any kind. For example, on Cathedral Peak there is a scattered growth of this pine, creeping like mosses over the roof, nowhere giving hint of an ascending axis. While, approached quite near, it still appears matty and heathy, and one experiences no difficulty in walking over the top of it, yet it is seldom absolutely prostrate, usually attaining a height of three or four feet with a main trunk, and with branches outspread above it, as if in ascending they had been checked by a ceiling against which they had been compelled to spread horizontally. The winter snow *is* a sort of ceiling, lasting half the year; while the pressed surface is made yet smoother by violent winds armed with cutting sand-grains that bear down any shoot which offers to rise much above the general level, and that carve the dead trunks and branches in beautiful patterns.

During stormy nights I have often camped snugly beneath the interlacing arches of this little pine. The needles, which have accumulated for centuries, make fine beds, a fact well known to other mountaineers, such as deer and wild sheep, who paw out oval hollows and lie beneath the larger trees in safe and comfortable concealment. This lowly dwarf reaches a far greater age than would be guessed. A specimen that I examined, growing at an elevation of 10,700 feet, yet looked as though it might be plucked up by the roots, for it was only three and a half inches in diameter and its topmost tassel reached hardly three feet above the ground. Cutting it half through and counting the annual rings with the aid of a lens, I found its age to be no less than 255 years. Another specimen about the same height, with a trunk six inches in diameter, I found to be 426 years old, forty years ago; and one of its supple branchlets hardly an eighth of an inch in diameter inside the bark, was seventy-five years old, and so filled with oily balsam and seasoned by storms that I tied it in knots like a whip-cord.

THE NUT PINE

In going across the Range from the Tuolumne River Soda Springs to Mono Lake one makes the acquaintance of the curious little

The Forest Trees in General

Nut Pine (*Pinus monophylla*). It dots the eastern flank of the Sierra to which it is mostly restricted in grayish bush-like patches, from the margin of the sage-plains to an elevation of from 7000 to 8000 feet. A more contented, fruitful and unaspiring conifer could not be conceived. All the species we have been sketching make departures more or less distant from the typical spire form, but none goes so far as this. Without any apparent cause it keeps near the ground, throwing out crooked, divergent branches like an orchard apple-tree, and seldom pushes a single shoot higher than fifteen or twenty feet above the ground.

The average thickness of the trunk is, perhaps, about ten or twelve inches. The leaves are mostly undivided, like round awls, instead of being separated, like those of other pines, into twos and threes and fives. The cones are green while growing, and are usually found over all the tree, forming quite a marked feature as seen against the bluish-gray foliage. They are quite small, only about two inches in length, and seem to have but little space for seeds; but when we come to open them, we find that about half the entire bulk of the cone is made up of sweet, nutritious nuts, nearly as large as hazel-nuts. This is undoubtedly the most important food-tree on the Sierra, and furnishes the Mona, Carson, and Walker River Indians with more and better nuts than all the other species taken together. It is the Indian's own tree, and many a white man have they killed for cutting it down. Being so low, the cones are readily beaten off with poles, and the nuts procured by roasting them until the scales open. In bountiful seasons a single Indian may gather thirty or forty bushels.

7

The Big Trees

BETWEEN the heavy pine and silver fir zones towers the Big Tree (*Sequoia gigantea*), the king of all the conifers in the world, "the noblest of the noble race." The groves nearest Yosemite Valley are about twenty miles to the westward and southward and are called the Tuolumne, Merced and Mariposa groves. It extends, a widely interrupted belt, from a very small grove on the middle fork of the American River to the head of Deer Creek, a distance of about 260 miles, its northern limit being near the thirty-ninth parallel, the southern a little below the thirty-sixth. The elevation of the belt above the sea varies from about 5000 to 8000 feet. From the American River to Kings River the species occurs only in small isolated groups so sparsely distributed along the belt that three of the gaps in it are from forty to sixty miles wide. But from Kings River southward the sequoia is not restricted to mere groves but extends across the wide rugged basins of the Kaweah and Tule Rivers in noble forests, a distance of nearly seventy miles, the continuity of this part of the belt being broken only by the main cañons. The Fresno, the largest of the northern groves, has an area of three or four square miles, a short distance to the southward of the famous Mariposa grove. Along the south rim of the cañon of the south fork of Kings River there is a majestic sequoia forest about six miles long by two wide. This is the northernmost group that may fairly be called a forest. Descending the divide between the Kings and Kaweah Rivers you come to the grand forests that form the main continuous portion of the belt. Southward the giants become more and more irrepressibly exuberant, heaving their massive crowns into the sky from every ridge and slope, waving onward in graceful compliance with the complicated topography of the region. The finest of the Kaweah section of the belt is on the broad ridge between Marble Creek and the middle fork, and is called the Giant Forest. It extends from the granite headlands, overlooking the hot San Joaquin plains, to within a few miles of the cool glacial fountains of the summit peaks. The extreme upper limit of the belt is reached between the middle and south forks of the Kaweah at a height of 8400 feet, but the finest block of big tree forests in the entire belt is on the north fork of Tule River, and is included in the Sequoia National Park.

In the northern groves there are comparatively few young trees or saplings. But here for every old storm-beaten giant there are many in their prime and for each of these a crowd of hopeful young trees and saplings, growing vigorously on moraines, rocky ledges, along water courses and meadows. But though the area occupied by the big tree increases so greatly from north to south, there is no marked increase in the size of the trees. The height of 275 feet or thereabouts and a diameter of about twenty feet, four feet from the ground is, perhaps, about the average size of what may be called full-grown trees, where they are favorably located. The specimens twenty-five feet in diameter are not very rare and a few are nearly three hundred feet high. In the Calaveras grove there are four trees over 300 feet in height, the tallest of which as measured by the Geological Survey is 325 feet. The very largest that I have yet met in the course of my explorations is a majestic old fire-scarred monument in the Kings River forest. It is thirty-five feet and eight inches in diameter inside the bark, four feet above the ground. It is burned half through, and I spent a day in clearing away the charred surface with a sharp ax and counting the annual wood-rings with the aid of a pocket lens. I succeeded in laying bare a section all the way from the outside to the heart and counted a little over four thousand rings, showing that this tree was in its prime about twenty-seven feet in diameter at the beginning of the Christian era. No other tree in the world, as far as I know, has looked down on so many centuries as the sequoia or opens so many impressive and suggestive views into history. Under the most favorable conditions these giants probably live 5000 years or more, though few of even the larger trees are half as old. The age of one that was felled in Calaveras grove, for the sake of having its stump for a dancing-floor, was about 1300 years, and its diameter measured across the stump twenty-four feet inside the bark. Another that was felled in the Kings River forest was about the same size but nearly a thousand years older (2200 years), though not a very old-looking tree.

So harmonious and finely balanced are even the mightiest of these monarchs in all their proportions that there is never anything overgrown or monstrous about them. Seeing them for the first time you are more impressed with their beauty than their size, their grandeur being in great part invisible; but sooner or later it becomes manifest to the loving eye, stealing slowly on the senses like the grandeur of Niagara or of the Yosemite Domes. When you approach them and walk around them you begin to wonder at their colossal size and try to measure them. They bulge considerably at the base, but not more than is required for beauty and safety and

The Big Trees

the only reason that this bulging seems in some cases excessive is that only a comparatively small section is seen in near views. One that I measured in the Kings River forest was twenty-five feet in diameter at the ground and ten feet in diameter 220 feet above the ground, showing the fineness of the taper of the trunk as a whole. No description can give anything like an adequate idea of their singular majesty, much less of their beauty. Except the sugar pine, most of their neighbors with pointed tops seem ever trying to go higher, while the big tree, soaring above them all, seems satisfied. Its grand domed head seems to be poised about as lightly as a cloud, giving no impression of seeking to rise higher. Only when it is young does it show like other conifers a heavenward yearning, sharply aspiring with a long quick-growing top. Indeed, the whole tree for the first century or two, or until it is a hundred or one hundred and fifty feet high, is arrowhead in form, and, compared with the solemn rigidity of age, seems as sensitive to the wind as a squirrel's tail. As it grows older, the lower branches are gradually dropped and the upper ones thinned out until comparatively few are left. These, however, are developed to a great size, divide again and again and terminate in bossy, rounded masses of leafy branchlets, while the head becomes dome-shaped, and is the first to feel the touch of the rosy beams of the morning, the last to bid the sun good night. Perfect specimens, unhurt by running fires or lightning, are singularly regular and symmetrical in general form, though not in the least conventionalized, for they show extraordinary variety in the unity and harmony of their general outline. The immensely strong, stately shafts are free of limbs for one hundred and fifty feet or so. The large limbs reach out with equal boldness in every direction, showing no weather side, and no other tree has

[97]

foliage so densely massed, so finely molded in outline and so perfectly subordinate to an ideal type. A particularly knotty, angular, ungovernable-looking branch, from five to seven or eight feet in diameter and perhaps a thousand years old, may occasionally be seen pushing out from the trunk as if determined to break across the bounds of the regular curve, but like all the others it dissolves in bosses of branchlets and sprays as soon as the general outline is approached. Except in picturesque old age, after being struck by lightning or broken by thousands of snow-storms, the regularity of forms is one of their most distinguishing characteristics. Another is the simple beauty of the trunk and its great thickness as compared with its height and the width of the branches, which makes them look more like finely modeled and sculptured architectural columns than the stems of trees, while the great limbs look like rafters, supporting the magnificent dome-head. But though so consummately beautiful, the big tree always seems unfamiliar, with peculiar physiognomy, awfully solemn and earnest; yet with all its strangeness it impresses us as being more at home than any of its neighbors, holding the best right to the ground as the oldest, strongest inhabitant. One soon becomes acquainted with new species of pine and fir and spruce as with friendly people, shaking their outstretched branches like shaking hands and fondling their little ones, while the venerable aboriginal sequoia, ancient of other days, keeps you at a distance, looking as strange in aspect and behavior among its neighbor trees as would the mastodon among the homely bears and deers. Only the Sierra juniper is at all like it, standing rigid and unconquerable on glacier pavements for thousands of years, grim and silent, with an air of antiquity about as pronounced as that of the sequoia.

The Big Trees

The bark of the largest trees is from one to two feet thick, rich cinnamon brown, purplish on young trees, forming magnificent masses of color with the underbrush. Toward the end of winter the trees are in bloom, while the snow is still eight or ten feet deep. The female flowers are about three-eighths of an inch long, pale green, and grow in countless thousands on the ends of sprays. The male are still more abundant, pale yellow, a fourth of an inch long and when the pollen is ripe they color the whole tree and dust the air and the ground. The cones are bright grass-green in color, about two and a half inches long, one and a half wide, made up of thirty or forty strong, closely-packed, rhomboidal scales, with four to eight seeds at the base of each. The seeds are wonderfully small and light, being only from an eighth to a fourth of an inch long and wide, including a filmy surrounding wing, which causes them to glint and waver in falling and enables the wind to carry them considerable distances. Unless harvested by the squirrels, the cones discharge their seed and remain on the tree for many years. In fruitful seasons the trees are fairly laden. On two small branches one and a half and two inches in diameter I counted 480 cones. No other California conifer produces nearly so many seeds, except, perhaps, the other sequoia, the Redwood of the Coast Mountains. Millions are ripened annually by a single tree, and in a fruitful year the product of one of the northern groves would be enough to plant all the mountain ranges in the world.

As soon as any accident happens to the crown, such as being smashed off by lightning, the branches beneath the wound, no matter how situated, seem to be excited, like a colony of bees that have lost their queen, and become anxious to repair the damage. Limbs that have grown outward for centuries at right angles to the trunk begin to turn upward to assist in making a new crown, each speedily assuming the special form of true summits. Even in the case of mere stumps, burned half through, some mere ornamental tuft will try to go aloft and do its best as a leader in forming a new head. Groups of two or three are often found standing close together, the seeds from which they sprang having probably grown on ground cleared for their reception by the fall of a large tree of a former generation. They are called "loving couples," "three graces," etc. When these trees are young they are seen to stand twenty or thirty feet apart, by the time they are full-grown their trunks will touch and crowd against each other and in some cases even appear as one.

It is generally believed that the sequoia was once far more widely distributed over the Sierra; but after long and careful study I have come to the conclusion that it never was, at least since the close of the glacial period, because a diligent search along the margins of the groves, and in the gaps between fails to reveal a single trace of its previous existence beyond its present bounds. Notwithstanding, I feel confident that if every sequoia in the Range were to die to-day, numerous monuments of their existence would remain, of so imperishable a nature as to be available for the student more than ten thousand years hence.

In the first place, no species of coniferous tree in the Range keeps its members so well together as the sequoia; a mile is, perhaps, the greatest distance of any straggler from the main body, and all of those stragglers that have come under my observation are young, instead of old monumental trees, relics of a more extended growth.

Again, the great trunks of the sequoia last for centuries after they fall. I have a specimen block of sequoia wood, cut from a fallen tree, which is hardly distinguishable from a similar section cut from a living tree, although the one cut from the fallen trunk has certainly lain on the damp forest floor more than 380 years, probably thrice as long. The time-measure in the case is simply this: When the ponderous trunk to which the old vestige belonged fell, it sunk itself into the ground, thus making a long, straight ditch, and in the middle of this ditch a silver fir four feet in diameter and 380 years old was growing, as I determined by cutting it half through and counting the rings, thus demonstrating that the remnant of the trunk that made the ditch has lain on the ground *more* than 380 years. For it is evident that, to find the whole time, we must add to the 380 years the time that the vanished portion of the trunk lay in the ditch before being burned out of the way, plus the time that passed before the seed from which the monumental fir sprang fell into the prepared soil and took root. Now, because sequoia trunks are never wholly consumed in one forest fire, and those fires recur only at considerable intervals, and because sequoia ditches after being cleared are often left unplanted for centuries, it becomes evident that the trunk-remnant in question may probably have lain a thousand years or more. And this instance is by no means a rare one.

Again, admitting that upon those areas supposed to have been once covered with sequoia forests, every tree may have fallen, and every trunk may have been burned or buried, leaving not a remnant, many of the ditches made by the fall of the ponderous trunks, and the bowls made by their upturning roots, would remain patent for thousands of years after the last vestige of the trunks that made them had vanished. Much of this ditch-writing would no doubt be quickly effaced by the flood-action of overflowing streams and rain-washing; but no inconsiderable portion would remain enduringly engraved on ridge-tops beyond such destructive action; for, where all the conditions are favorable, it is almost imperishable. Now these historic ditches and root-bowls occur in all the present sequoia groves and forests, but, as far as I have observed, not the faintest vestige of one presents itself outside of them.

We therefore conclude that the area covered by sequoia has not been diminished during the last eight or ten thousand years, and probably not at all in post-glacial time. Nevertheless, the questions may be asked: Is the species verging toward extinction? What are its relations to climate, soil, and associated trees?

All the phenomena bearing on these questions also throw light, as we shall endeavor to show, upon the peculiar distribution of the species, and sustain the conclusion already arrived at as to the question of former extension. In the northern groups, as we have seen, there are few young trees or saplings growing up around the old ones to perpetuate the race, and inasmuch as those aged sequoias, so nearly childless, are the only ones commonly known, the species, to most observers, seems doomed to speedy extinction, as being nothing more than an expiring remnant, vanquished in the so-called struggle for life by pines and firs that have driven it into its last strongholds in moist glens where the climate is supposed to be exceptionally favorable. But the story told by the majestic continuous forests of the south creates a very different impression. No tree in the forest is more enduringly established in concordance with both climate and soil. It grows heartily everywhere—on moraines, rocky ledges, along watercourses, and in the deep, moist alluvium of meadows with, as we have seen, a multi-

The Big Trees

tude of seedlings and saplings crowding up around the aged, abundantly able to maintain the forest in prime vigor. So that if all the trees of any section of the main sequoia forest were ranged together according to age, a very promising curve would be presented, all the way up from last year's seedlings to giants, and with the young and middle-aged portion of the curve many times longer than the old portion. Even as far north as the Fresno, I counted 536 saplings and seedlings, growing promisingly upon a landslip not exceeding two acres in area. This soil-bed was about seven years old, and had been seeded almost simultaneously by pines, firs, libocedrus, and sequoia, presenting a simple and instructive illustration of the struggle for life among the rival species; and it was interesting to note that the conditions thus far affecting them have enabled the young sequoias to gain a marked advantage. Toward the south where the sequoia becomes most exuberant and numerous, the rival trees become less so; and where they mix with sequoias they grow up beneath them like slender grasses among stalks of Indian corn. Upon a bed of sandy floodsoil I counted ninety-four sequoias, from one to twelve feet high, on a patch of ground once occupied by four large sugar pines which lay crumbling beneath them—an instance of conditions which have enabled sequoias to crowd out the pines. I also noted eighty-six vigorous saplings upon a piece of fresh ground prepared for their reception by fire. Thus fire, the great destroyer of the sequoia, also furnishes the bare ground required for its growth from the seed. Fresh ground is, however, furnished in sufficient quantities for the renewal of the forests without the aid of fire—by the fall of old trees. The soil is thus upturned and mellowed, and many trees are planted for every one that falls.

The Yosemite

It is constantly asserted in a vague way that the Sierra was vastly wetter than now, and that the increasing drought will of itself extinguish the sequoia, leaving its ground to other trees supposed capable of flourishing in a drier climate. But that the sequoia can and does grow on as dry ground as any of its present rivals is manifest in a thousand places. "Why, then," it will be asked, "are sequoias always found only in well-watered places?" Simply because a growth of sequoias creates those streams. The thirsty mountaineer knows well that in every sequoia grove he will find running water, but it is a mistake to suppose that the water is the cause of the grove being there; on the contrary, the grove is the cause of the water being there. Drain off the water and the trees will remain, but cut off the trees, and the streams will vanish. Never was cause more completely mistaken for effect than in the case of these related phenomena of sequoia woods and perennial streams.

When attention is called to the method of sequoia stream-making, it will be apprehended at once. The roots of this immense tree fill the ground, forming a thick sponge that absorbs and holds back the rain and melting snow, only allowing it to ooze and flow gently. Indeed, every fallen leaf and rootlet, as well as long clasping root, and prostrate trunk, may be regarded as a dam hoarding the bounty of storm-clouds, and dispensing it as blessings all through the summer, instead of allowing it to go headlong in short-lived floods.

Since, then, it is a fact that thousands of sequoias are growing thriftily on what is termed dry ground, and even clinging like mountain pines to rifts in granite precipices, and since it has also been shown that the extra moisture found in connection with the denser growths is an effect of their presence, instead of a cause of their presence, then the notions as to the former extension of the species and its near approach to extinction, based upon its supposed dependence on greater moisture, are seen to be erroneous.

The decrease in rain and snowfall since the close of the glacial period in the Sierra is much less than is commonly guessed. The highest post-glacial water-marks are well preserved in all the upper river channels, and they are not greatly higher than the spring flood-marks of the present; showing conclusively that no extraordinary decrease has taken place in the volume of the upper tributaries of post-glacial Sierra streams since they came into existence. But, in the meantime, eliminating all this complicated question of climatic change, the plain fact remains that the present rain and snowfall is abundantly sufficient for the luxuriant growth of sequoia forests. Indeed, all my observations tend to show that in a prolonged drought the sugar pines and firs would perish before the sequoia, not alone because of the greater longevity of individual trees, but because the species can endure more drought, and make the most of whatever moisture falls.

Again, if the restriction and irregular distribution of the species be interpreted as a result of the desiccation of the Range, then instead of increasing as it does in individuals toward the south where the rainfall is less, it should diminish. If, then, the peculiar distribution of sequoia has not been governed by superior conditions of soil as to fertility or moisture, by what has it been governed?

In the course of my studies I observed that the northern groves, the only ones I was at first acquainted with, were located on just those portions of the general forest soil-belt that were first laid bare toward the close of the glacial period when the ice-sheet began to break up into individual glaciers. And while searching the wide basin of the San Joaquin, and trying to account for the absence of sequoia where every condition seemed favorable for its growth, it occurred to me that this remarkable gap in the sequoia belt fifty miles wide is located exactly in the basin of the vast, ancient *mer de glace* of the San Joaquin and Kings River basins which poured its frozen floods to the plain through this gap as its channel. I then perceived that the next great gap in the belt to the northward, forty miles wide, extending between the Calaveras and Tuolumne groves, occurs in the basin of the great ancient mer de glace of the Tuolumne and Stanislaus basins; and that the smaller gap between the Merced and Mariposa groves occurs in the basin of the smaller glacier of the Merced. The wider the ancient glacier, the wider the corresponding gap in the sequoia belt.

Finally, pursuing my investigations across the basins of the Kaweah and Tule, I discovered that the sequoia belt attained its greatest development just where, owing to the topographical peculiarities of the region, the ground had been best protected from the main ice-rivers that continued to pour past from the summit fountains long after the smaller local glaciers had been melted.

Taking now a general view of the belt, beginning at the south, we see that the majestic ancient glaciers were shed off right and left down the valleys of Kern and Kings Rivers by the lofty protective spurs outspread embracingly above the warm sequoia-filled basins of the Kaweah and Tule. Then, next northward, occurs the wide sequoia-less channel, or basin of the ancient San Joaquin and Kings River mer de glace; then the warm, protected spots of Fresno and Mariposa groves; then the sequoia-less channel of the ancient Merced glacier; next the warm, sheltered ground of the Merced and Tuolumne groves; then the sequoia-less channel of the grand ancient mer de glace of the Tuolumne and Stanislaus; then the warm old ground of the Calaveras and Stanislaus groves. It appears, therefore, that just where, at a certain period in the history of the Sierra, the glaciers were not, there the sequoia is, and just where the glaciers were, there the sequoia is not.

But although all the observed phenomena bearing on the post-glacial history of this colossal tree point to the conclusion that it never was more widely distributed on the Sierra since the close of the glacial epoch; that its present forests are scarcely past prime, if, indeed, they have reached prime; that the post-glacial day of the species is probably not half done; yet, when from a wider outlook the vast antiquity of the genus is considered, and its ancient richness in species and individuals,—comparing our Sierra Giant and *Sequoia sempervirens* of the Coast Range, the only other living species of sequoia, with the twelve fossil species already discovered and described by Heer and Lesquereux, some of which flourished over vast areas in the Arctic regions and in Europe and our own territories, during tertiary and cretaceous times—then, indeed, it becomes plain that our two surviving species, restricted to narrow belts within the limits of California, are mere remnants of the genus, both as to species and individuals, and that they may be verging to extinction. But the verge of a period beginning in cretaceous times may have a breadth of tens of thousands of years, not to mention the possible existence of conditions calculated to multiply and re-extend both species and individuals.

There is no absolute limit to the existence of any tree. Death is due to accidents, not, as that of animals, to the wearing out of organs. Only the leaves die of old age. Their fall is foretold in their structure; but the leaves are renewed every year, and so also are the essential organs—wood, roots, bark, buds. Most of the Sierra trees die of disease, insects, fungi, etc., but nothing hurts the big tree. I never saw one that was sick or showed the slightest sign of decay. Barring accidents, it seems to be immortal. It is a curious fact that all the very old sequoias had lost their heads by lightning strokes. "All things come to him who waits." But of all living things, sequoia is perhaps the only one able to wait long enough to make sure of being struck by lightning.

So far as I am able to see at present only fire and the ax threaten the existence of these noblest of God's trees. In Nature's keeping they are safe, but through the agency of man destruction is making rapid progress, while in the work of protection only a good beginning has been made. The Fresno grove, the Tuolumne, Merced and Mariposa groves are under the protection of the Federal Government in the Yosemite National Park. So are the General Grant and Sequoia National Parks; the latter, established twenty-one years ago, has an area of 240 square miles and is efficiently guarded by a troop of cavalry under the direction of the Secretary of the Interior; so also are the small General Grant National Park, established at the same time with an area of four square miles, and the Mariposa grove, about the same size and the small Merced and Tuolumne group. Perhaps more than half of all the big trees have been thoughtlessly sold and are now in the hands of speculators and mill men. It appears, therefore, that far the largest and important section of protected big trees is in the great Sequoia National Park, now easily accessible by rail to Lemon Cove and thence by a good stage road into the giant forest of the Kaweah and thence by trail to other parts of the park; but large as it is it should be made much larger. Its natural eastern boundary is the High Sierra and the northern and southern boundaries are the Kings and Kern Rivers. Thus could be included the sublime scenery on the headwaters of these rivers and perhaps nine-tenths of all the big trees in existence. All private claims within these bounds should be gradually extinguished by purchase by the Government. The big tree, leaving all its higher uses out of the count, is a tree of life to the dwellers of the plain dependent on irrigation, a never-failing spring, sending living waters to the lowland. For every grove cut down a stream is dried up. Therefore all California is crying, "Save the trees of the fountains." Nor, judging by the signs of the times, is it likely that the cry will cease until the salvation of all that is left of *Sequoia gigantea* is made sure.

8

The Flowers

YOSEMITE was all one glorious flower garden before plows and scythes and trampling, biting horses came to make its wide open spaces look like farmers' pasture fields. Nevertheless, countless flowers still bloom every year in glorious profusion on the grand talus slopes, wall benches and tablets, and in all the fine, cool side-cañons up to the rim of the Valley, and beyond, higher and higher, to the summits of the peaks. Even on the open floor and in easily-reached side-nooks many common flowering plants have survived and still make a brave show in the spring and early summer. Among these we may mention tall œnotheras, *Pentstemon lutea*, and *P. Douglasii* with fine blue and red flowers; Spraguea, scarlet zauschneria, with its curious radiant rosettes characteristic of the sandy flats; mimulus, eunanus, blue and white violets, geranium, columbine, erythraea, larkspur, collomia, draperia, gilias, heleniums, bahia, goldenrods, daisies, honeysuckle; heuchera, bolandra, saxifrages, gentians; in cool cañon nooks and on Clouds' Rest and the base of Starr King Dome you may find *Primula suffrutescens*, the only wild primrose discovered in California, and the only known shrubby species in the genus. And there are several fine orchids, habenaria, and cypripedium, the latter very rare, once common in the Valley near the foot of Glacier Point, and in a bog on the rim of the Valley near a place called Gentry's Station, now abandoned. It is a very beautiful species,

The Flowers

the large oval lip white, delicately veined with purple; the other petals and the sepals purple, strap-shaped, and elegantly curled and twisted.

Of the lily family, fritillaria, smilacina, chlorogalum and several fine species of brodiæa, Ithuriel's spear, and others less prized are common, and the favorite calochortus, or Mariposa lily, a unique genus of many species, something like the tulips of Europe but far finer. Most of them grow on the warm foothills below the Valley, but two charming species, C. cœruleus and C. nudus, dwell in springy places on the Wawona road a few miles beyond the brink of the walls.

The snow plant (*Sarcodes sanguinea*) is more admired by tourists than any other in California. It is red, fleshy and watery and looks like a gigantic asparagus shoot. Soon after the snow is off the ground it rises through the dead needles and humus in the pine and fir woods like a bright glowing pillar of fire. In a week or so it grows to a height of eight or twelve inches with a diameter of an inch and a half or two inches; then its long fringed bracts curl aside, allowing the twenty- or thirty-five-lobed, bell-shaped flowers to open and look straight out from the axis. It is said to grow up through the snow; on the contrary, it always waits until the ground is warm, though with other early flowers it is occasionally buried or half-buried for a day or two by spring storms. The entire plant— flowers, bracts, stem, scales, and roots—is fiery red. Its color should appeal to one's blood. Nevertheless, it is a singularly cold and unsympathetic plant. Everybody admires it as a wonderful curiosity, but nobody loves it as lilies, violets, roses, daisies are loved. Without fragrance, it stands beneath the pines and firs lonely and silent, as if unacquainted with any other plant in the world; never moving in the wildest storms; rigid as if lifeless, though covered with beautiful rosy flowers.

Far the most delightful and fragrant of the Valley flowers is the Washington lily, white, moderate in size, with from three- to ten-flowered racemes. I found one specimen in the lower end of the Valley at the foot of the Wawona grade that was eight feet high, the raceme two feet long, with fifty-two flowers, fifteen of them open; the others had faded or were still in the bud. This famous lily is distributed over the sunny portions of the sugar-pine woods, never in large meadow-garden companies like the large and the small tiger lilies (*pardalinum* and *parvum*), but widely scattered, standing up to the waist in dense ceanothus and manzanita chaparral, waving its lovely flowers above the blooming wilderness of brush, and giving their fragrance to the breeze. It is now becoming scarce in the most accessible parts of its range on account of the high price paid for its bulbs by gardeners through whom it has been distributed far and wide over the flower-loving world. For, on account of its pure color and delicate, delightful fragrance, all lily lovers at once adopted it as a favorite.

The principal shrubs are manzanita and ceanothus, several species of each, azalea, *Rubus nutkanus*, brier rose, choke-cherry, philadelphus, calycanthus, garrya, rhamnus, etc.

The manzanita never fails to attract particular attention. The species common in the Valley is usually about six or seven feet high, round-headed with innumerable branches, red or chocolate-color bark, pale green leaves set on edge, and a rich profusion of small, pink, narrow-throated, urn-shaped flowers, like those of arbutus. The knotty, crooked, angular branches are about as rigid as bones, and the red bark is so thin and smooth on both trunk and

The Flowers

branches, they look as if they had been peeled and polished and painted. In the spring large areas on the mountain up to a height of eight or nine thousand feet are brightened with the rosy flowers, and in autumn with their red fruit. The pleasantly acid berries, about the size of peas, look like little apples, and a hungry mountaineer is glad to eat them, though half their bulk is made up of hard seeds. Indians, bears, coyotes, foxes, birds and other mountain people live on them for weeks and months. The different species of ceanothus usually associated with manzanita are flowery fragrant and altogether delightful shrubs, growing in glorious abundance, not only in the Valley, but high up in the forest on sunny or half-shaded ground. In the sugar-pine woods the most beautiful species is C. *integerrimus*, often called Californian lilac, or deer brush. It is five or six feet high with slender branches, glossy foliage, and abundance of blue flowers in close, showy panicles. Two species, C. *prostratus* and C. *procumbens*, spread smooth, blue-flowered mats and rugs beneath the pines, and offer fine beds to tired mountaineers. The commonest species, C. *cordulatus*, is most common in the silver-fir woods. It is white-flowered and thorny, and makes dense thickets of tangled chaparral, difficult to wade through or to walk over. But it is pressed flat every winter by ten or fifteen feet of snow. The western azalea makes glorious beds of bloom along the river bank and meadows. In the Valley it is from two to five feet high, has fine green leaves, mostly hidden beneath its rich profusion of large, fragrant white and yellow flowers, which are in their prime in June, July and August, according to the elevation, ranging from 3000 to 6000 feet. Near the azalea-bordered streams the small wild rose, resembling R. *blanda*, makes large thickets deliciously fragrant, especially on a dewy morning and

[113]

after showers. Not far from these azalea and rose gardens, *Rubus nutkanus* covers the ground with broad, soft, velvety leaves, and pure-white flowers as large as those of its neighbor and relative, the rose, and much finer in texture, followed at the end of summer by soft red berries good for everybody. This is the commonest and the most beautiful of the whole blessed, flowery, fruity Rubus genus.

There are a great many interesting ferns in the Valley and about it. Naturally enough the greater number are rock ferns— pellæa, cheilanthes, polypodium, adiantum, woodsia, cryptogramma, etc., with small tufted fronds, lining cool glens and fringing the seams of the cliffs. The most important of the larger species are woodwardia, aspidium, asplenium, and, above all, the common pteris. *Woodwardia radicans* is a superb, broad-shouldered fern five to eight feet high, growing in vase-shaped clumps where the ground is nearly level and on some of the benches of the north wall of the Valley where it is watered by a broad trickling stream. It thatches the sloping rocks, frond overlapping frond like roof shingles. The broad-fronded, hardy *Pteris aquilina*, the commonest of ferns, covers large areas on the floor of the Valley. No other fern does so much for the color glory of autumn, with its browns and reds and yellows, even after lying dead beneath the snow all winter. It spreads a rich brown mantle over the desolate ground in the spring before the grass has sprouted, and at the first touch of sun-heat its young fronds come rearing up full of faith and hope through the midst of the last year's ruins.

Of the five species of pellæa, *P. Breweri* is the hardiest as to enduring high altitudes and stormy weather and at the same time it is the most fragile of the genus. It grows in dense tufts in the clefts of storm-beaten rocks, high up on the mountain-side on the very edge of the fern line. It is a handsome little fern about four or five inches high, has pale-green pinnate fronds, and shining bronze-colored stalks about as brittle as glass. Its companions on the lower part of its range are *Cryptogramma acrostichoides* and *Phegopteris alpestris*, the latter with soft, delicate fronds, not in the least like those of Rock fern, though it grows on the rocks where the snow lies longest. *Pellaea Bridgesii*, with blue-green, narrow, simply-pinnate fronds, is about the same size as Breweri and ranks next to it as a mountaineer, growing in fissures, wet or dry, and around the edges of boulders that are resting on glacier pavements with no fissures whatever. About a thousand feet lower we find the smaller, more abundant *P. densa* on ledges and boulder-strewn, fissured pavements, watered until late in summer from oozing currents, derived from lingering snowbanks. It is, or rather was, extremely abundant between the foot of the Nevada and the head of the Vernal Fall, but visitors with great industry have dug out almost every root, so that now one has to scramble in out-of-the-way places to find it. The three species of Cheilanthes in the Valley—*C. californica, C. gracillima*, and *myriophylla*, with beautiful two-to-four-pinnate fronds, an inch to five inches long, adorn the stupendous walls however dry and sheer. The exceedingly delicate californica is so rare that I have found it only once. The others are abundant and are sometimes accompanied by the little gold fern, *Gymnogramme triangularis*, and rarely by the curious little *Botrychium simplex*, some of them less than an inch high. The finest of all the rock ferns is *Adiantum pedatum*, lover of waterfalls and the finest spray-dust. The homes it loves best are over-leaning, cave-like hollows, beside the larger falls, where it can wet its fingers with their dewy spray. Many of these moss-lined chambers contain thousands of these delightful ferns, clinging to mossy walls by the slightest hold, reaching out their delicate finger-fronds on dark, shining stalks, sensitive and tremulous, throbbing in unison with every movement and tone of the falling water, moving each division of the frond separately at times, as if fingering the music.

May and June are the main bloom-months of the year. Both the flowers and falls are then at their best. By the first of August the midsummer glories of the Valley are past their prime. The young birds are then out of their nests. Most of the plants have gone to seed; berries are ripe; autumn tints begin to kindle and burn over meadow and grove, and a soft mellow haze in the morning sunbeams heralds the approach of Indian summer. The shallow river is now at rest, its flood-work done. It is now but little more than a series of pools united by trickling, whispering currents that steal softly over brown pebbles and sand with scarce an audible murmur. Each pool has a character of its own and, though they are nearly currentless, the night air and tree shadows keep them cool. Their shores curve in and out in bay and promontory, giving the appearance of miniature lakes, their banks in most places embossed with brier and azalea, sedge and grass and fern; and above these in their glory of autumn colors a mingled growth of alder, willow, dogwood and balm-of-Gilead; mellow sunshine overhead, cool shadows beneath; light filtered and strained in passing through the ripe leaves like that which passes through colored windows. The surface of the water is stirred, perhaps, by whirling water-beetles, or some startled trout, seeking shelter beneath fallen logs or roots. The falls, too, are quiet; no wind stirs, and the whole Valley floor is a mosaic of greens and purples, yellows and reds. Even the rocks seem strangely soft and mellow, as if they, too, had ripened.

9

The Birds

THE songs of the Yosemite winds and waterfalls are delightfully enriched with bird song, especially in the nesting time of spring and early summer. The most familiar and best known of all is the common robin, who may be seen every day, hopping about briskly on the meadows and uttering his cheery, enlivening call. The black-headed grosbeak, too, is here, with the Bullock oriole, and western tanager, brown song-sparrow, hermit thrush, the purple finch,—a fine singer, with head and throat of a rosy-red hue,— several species of warblers and vireos, kinglets, flycatchers, etc.

But the most wonderful singer of all the birds is the water-ouzel that dives into foaming rapids and feeds at the bottom, holding on in a wonderful way, living a charmed life.

Several species of humming-birds are always to be seen, darting and buzzing among the showy flowers. The little red-bellied nuthatches, the chickadees, and little brown creepers, threading the furrows of the bark of the pines, searching for food in the crevices. The large Steller's jay makes merry in the pine-tops; flocks of beautiful green swallows skim over the streams, and the noisy Clarke's crow may oftentimes be seen on the highest points around the Valley; and in the deep woods beyond the walls you may frequently hear and see the dusky grouse and the pileated woodpecker, or woodcock almost as large as a pigeon. The junco or snow-bird builds its nest on the floor of the Valley among the ferns;

several species of sparrow are common and the beautiful lazuli bunting, a common bird in the underbrush, flitting about among the azalea and ceanothus bushes and enlivening the groves with his brilliant color; and on gravelly bars the spotted sandpiper is sometimes seen. Many woodpeckers dwell in the Valley; the familiar flicker, the Harris woodpecker and the species which so busily stores up acorns in the thick bark of the yellow pines.

The short, cold days of winter are also sweetened with the music and hopeful chatter of a considerable number of birds. No cheerier choir ever sang in snow. First and best of all is the water-ouzel, a dainty, dusky little bird about the size of a robin, that sings a sweet fluty song all winter and all summer, in storms and calms, sunshine and shadow, haunting the rapids and waterfalls with marvelous constancy, building his nest in the cleft of a rock bathed in spray. He is not web-footed, yet he dives fearlessly into foaming rapids, seeming to take the greater delight the more boisterous the stream, always as cheerful and calm as any linnet in a grove. All his gestures as he flits about amid the loud uproar of the falls bespeak the utmost simplicity and confidence—bird and stream one and inseparable. What a pair! yet they are well related. A finer bloom than the foam bell in an eddying pool is this little bird. We may miss the meaning of the loud-resounding torrent, but the flute-like voice of the bird—only love is in it.

A few robins, belated on their way down from the upper meadows, linger in the Valley and make out to spend the winter in comparative comfort, feeding on the mistletoe berries that grow on the oaks. In the depths of the great forests, on the high meadows, in the severest altitudes, they seem as much at home as in the fields and orchards about the busy habitations of man, ascending the

The Birds

Sierra as the snow melts, following the green footsteps of Spring, until in July or August the highest glacier meadows are reached on the summit of the Range. Then, after the short summer is over, and their work in cheering and sweetening these lofty wilds is done, they gradually make their way down again in accord with the weather, keeping below the snow-storms, lingering here and there to feed on huckleberries and frost-nipped wild cherries growing on the upper slopes. Thence down to the vineyards and orchards of the lowlands to spend the winter; entering the gardens of the great towns as well as parks and fields, where the blessed wanderers are too often slaughtered for food—surely a bad use to put so fine a musician to; better make stove wood of pianos to feed the kitchen fire.

The kingfisher winters in the Valley, and the flicker and, of course, the carpenter woodpecker, that lays up large stores of acorns in the bark of trees; wrens also, with a few brown and gray linnets, and flocks of the arctic bluebird, making lively pictures among the snow-laden mistletoe bushes. Flocks of pigeons are often seen, and about six species of ducks, as the river is never wholly frozen over. Among these are the mallard and the beautiful woodduck, now less common on account of being so often shot at. Flocks of wandering geese used to visit the Valley in March and April, and perhaps do so still, driven down by hunger or stress of weather while on their way across the Range. When pursued by the hunters I have frequently seen them try to fly over the walls of the Valley until tired out and compelled to re-alight. Yosemite magnitudes seem to be as deceptive to geese as to men, for after circling to a considerable height and forming regular harrow-shaped ranks they would suddenly find themselves in danger of being dashed against the face of the cliff, much nearer the bottom than the top. Then turning in confusion with loud screams they would try again and again until exhausted and compelled to descend. I have occasionally observed large flocks on their travels crossing the summits of the Range at a height of 12,000 to 13,000 feet above the level of the sea, and even in so rare an atmosphere as this they seemed to be sustaining themselves without extra effort. Strong, however, as they are of wind and wing, they cannot fly over Yosemite walls, starting from the bottom.

A pair of golden eagles have lived in the Valley ever since I first visited it, hunting all winter along the northern cliffs and down the river cañon. Their nest is on a ledge of the cliff over which pours the Nevada Fall. Perched on the top of a dead spar, they were always interested observers of the geese when they were being shot at. I once noticed one of the geese compelled to leave the flock on account of being sorely wounded, although it still seemed to fly pretty well. Immediately the eagles pursued it and no doubt struck it down, although I did not see the result of the hunt. Anyhow, it flew past me up the Valley, closely pursued.

One wild, stormy winter morning after five feet of snow had fallen on the floor of the Valley and the flying flakes driven by a strong wind still thickened the air, making darkness like the approach of night, I sallied forth to see what I might learn and enjoy. It was impossible to go very far without the aid of snow-shoes, but I found no great difficulty in making my way to a part of the river where one of my ouzels lived. I found him at home busy about his breakfast, apparently unaware of anything uncomfortable in the weather. Presently he flew out to a stone against which the icy current was beating, and turning his back to the wind, sang as delightfully as a lark in springtime.

The Birds

After spending an hour or two with my favorite, I made my way across the Valley, boring and wallowing through the loose snow, to learn as much as possible about the way the other birds were spending their time. In winter one can always find them because they are then restricted to the north side of the Valley, especially the Indian Cañon groves, which from their peculiar exposure are the warmest.

I found most of the robins cowering on the lee side of the larger branches of the trees, where the snow could not fall on them, while two or three of the more venturesome were making desperate efforts to get at the mistletoe berries by clinging to the underside of the snow-crowned masses, back downward, something like woodpeckers. Every now and then some of the loose snow was dislodged and sifted down on the hungry birds, sending them screaming back to their companions in the grove, shivering and muttering like cold, hungry children.

Some of the sparrows were busy scratching and pecking at the feet of the larger trees where the snow had been shed off, gleaning seeds and benumbed insects, joined now and then by a robin weary of his unsuccessful efforts to get at the snow-covered mistletoe berries. The brave woodpeckers were clinging to the snowless sides of the larger boles and overarching branches of the camp trees, making short flights from side to side of the grove, pecking now and then at the acorns they had stored in the bark, and chattering aimlessly as if unable to keep still, evidently putting in the time in a very dull way. The hardy nuthatches were threading the open furrows of the barks in their usual industrious manner and uttering their quaint notes, giving no evidence of distress. The Steller's jays were, of course, making more noise and stir than all the other birds combined; ever coming and going with loud bluster, screaming as if each had a lump of melting sludge in his throat, and taking good care to improve every opportunity afforded by the darkness and confusion of the storm to steal from the acorn stores of the wood-peckers. One of the golden eagles made an impressive picture as he stood bolt upright on the top of a tall pine-stump, braving the storm, with his back to the wind and a tuft of snow piled on his broad shoulders, a monument of passive endurance. Thus every storm-bound bird seemed more or less uncomfortable, if not in distress. The storm was reflected in every gesture, and not one cheerful note, not to say song, came from a single bill. Their cowering, joyless endurance offered striking contrasts to the sponta-neous, irrepressible gladness of the ouzel, who could no more help giving out sweet song than a rose sweet fragrance. He must sing, though the heavens fall.

10

The South Dome

WITH the exception of a few spires and pinnacles, the South Dome is the only rock about the Valley that is strictly inaccessible without artificial means, and its inaccessibility is expressed in severe terms. Nevertheless many a mountaineer, gazing admiringly, tried hard to invent a way to the top of its noble crown—all in vain, until in the year 1875, George Anderson, an indomitable Scotchman, undertook the adventure. The side facing Tenaya Cañon is an absolutely vertical precipice from the summit to a depth of about 1600 feet, and on the opposite side it is nearly vertical for about as great a depth. The southwest side presents a very steep and finely drawn curve from the top down a thousand feet or more, while on the northeast, where it is united with the Clouds' Rest Ridge, one may easily reach a point called the Saddle, about seven hundred feet below the summit. From the Saddle the Dome rises in a graceful curve a few degrees too steep for unaided climbing, besides being defended by overleaning ends of the concentric dome layers of the granite.

A year or two before Anderson gained the summit, John Conway, the master trail-builder of the Valley, and his little sons, who climbed smooth rocks like lizards, made a bold effort to reach the top by climbing barefooted up the grand curve with a rope which they fastened at irregular intervals by means of eye-bolts driven into joints of the rock. But finding that the upper part would re-

quire laborious drilling, they abandoned the attempt, glad to escape from the dangerous position they had reached, some 300 feet
above the Saddle. Anderson began with Conway's old rope, which
had been left in place, and resolutely drilled his way to the top,
inserting eye-bolts five to six feet apart, and making his rope fast to
each in succession, resting his feet on the last bolt while he drilled
a hole for the next above. Occasionally some irregularity in the
curve, or slight foothold, would enable him to climb a few feet
without a rope, which he would pass and begin drilling again, and
thus the whole work was accomplished in a few days. From this
slender beginning he proposed to construct a substantial stairway
which he hoped to complete in time for the next year's travel, but
while busy getting out timber for his stairway and dreaming of the
wealth he hoped to gain from tolls, he was taken sick and died all
alone in his little cabin.

On the 10th of November, after returning from a visit to
Mount Shasta, a month or two after Anderson had gained the summit, I made haste to the Dome, not only for the pleasure of climbing, but to see what I might learn. The first winter storm-clouds
had blossomed and the mountains and all the high points about
the Valley were mantled in fresh snow. I was, therefore, a little
apprehensive of danger from the slipperiness of the rope and the
rock. Anderson himself tried to prevent me from making the attempt, refusing to believe that any one could climb his rope in the
snow-muffled condition in which it then was. Moreover, the sky
was overcast and solemn snow-clouds began to curl around the
summit, and my late experiences on icy Shasta came to mind. But
reflecting that I had matches in my pocket, and that a little fire-
wood might be found, I concluded that in case of a storm the night

could be spent on the Dome without suffering anything worth minding, no matter what the clouds might bring forth. I therefore pushed on and gained the top.

It was one of those brooding, changeful days that come between Indian summer and winter, when the leaf colors have grown dim and the clouds come and go among the cliffs like living creatures looking for work: now hovering aloft, now caressing rugged rock-brows with great gentleness, or, wandering afar over the tops of the forests, touching the spires of fir and pine with their soft silken fringes as if trying to tell the glad news of the coming of snow.

The first view was perfectly glorious. A massive cloud of pure pearl luster, apparently as fixed and calm as the meadows and groves in the shadow beneath it, was arched across the Valley from wall to wall, one end resting on the grand abutment of El Capitan, the other on Cathedral Rock. A little later, as I stood on the tremendous verge overlooking Mirror Lake, a flock of smaller clouds, white as snow, came from the north, trailing their downy skirts over the dark forests, and entered the Valley with solemn god-like gestures through Indian Cañon and over the North Dome and Royal Arches, moving swiftly, yet with majestic deliberation. On they came, nearer and nearer, gathering and massing beneath my feet and filling the Tenaya Cañon. Then the sun shone free, lighting the pearly gray surface of the cloud-like sea and making it glow. Gazing, admiring, I was startled to see for the first time the rare optical phenomenon of the "Specter of the Brocken." My shadow, clearly outlined, about half a mile long, lay upon this glorious white surface with startling effect. I walked back and forth, waved my arms and struck all sorts of attitudes, to see every slightest movement enormously exaggerated. Considering that I have looked down so many times from mountain tops on seas of all sorts of clouds, it seems strange that I should have seen the "Brocken Specter" only this once. A grander surface and a grander standpoint, however, could hardly have been found in all the Sierra.

After this grand show the cloud-sea rose higher, wreathing the Dome, and for a short time submerging it, making darkness like night, and I began to think of looking for a camp ground in a cluster of dwarf pines. But soon the sun shone free again, the clouds, sinking lower and lower, gradually vanished, leaving the Valley with its Indian-summer colors apparently refreshed, while to the eastward the summit-peaks, clad in new snow, towered along the horizon in glorious array.

Though apparently it is perfectly bald, there are four clumps of pines growing on the summit, representing three species, Pinus albicaulis, P. contorta and P. ponderosa, var. Jeffreyi—all three, of course, repressed and storm-beaten. The alpine spiræa grows here also and blossoms profusely with potentilla, erigeron, eriogonum, pentstemon, solidago, and an interesting species of onion, and four or five species of grasses and sedges. None of these differs in any respect from those of other summits of the same height, excepting the curious little narrow-leaved, waxen-bulbed onion, which I had not seen elsewhere.

Notwithstanding the enthusiastic eagerness of tourists to reach the crown of the Dome the views of the Valley from this lofty standpoint are less striking than from many other points comparatively low, chiefly on account of the foreshortening effect produced by looking down from so great a height. The North Dome is dwarfed almost beyond recognition, the grand sculpture of the Royal Arches is scarcely noticeable, and the whole range of walls on both sides seem comparatively low, especially when the Valley is flooded with noon sunshine; while the Dome itself, the most sublime feature of all the Yosemite views, is out of sight beneath one's feet. The view of Little Yosemite Valley is very fine, though inferior to one obtained from the base of the Starr King Cone, but the summit landscapes towards Mounts Ritter, Lyell, Dana, Conness, and the Merced Group, are very effective and complete.

No one has attempted to carry out Anderson's plan of making the Dome accessible. For my part I should prefer leaving it in pure wildness, though, after all, no great damage could be done by tramping over it. The surface would be strewn with tin cans and bottles, but the winter gales would blow the rubbish away. Avalanches might strip off any sort of stairway or ladder that might be built. Blue jays and Clark's crows have trodden the Dome for many a day, and so have beetles and chipmunks, and Tissiack would hardly be more "conquered" or spoiled should man be added to her list of visitors. His louder scream and heavier scrambling would not stir a line of her countenance.

When the sublime ice-floods of the glacial period poured down the flank of the Range over what is now Yosemite Valley, they were compelled to break through a dam of domes extending across from Mount Starr King to North Dome; and as the period began to draw near a close the shallowing ice-currents were divided and the South Dome was, perhaps, the first to emerge, burnished and shining like a mirror above the surface of the icy sea; and though it has sustained the wear and tear of the elements tens of thousands of years, it yet remains a telling monument of the action of the great glaciers that brought it to light. Its entire surface is still covered with glacial hieroglyphics whose interpretation is the reward of all who devoutly study them.

11

The Ancient Yosemite Glaciers:
How the Valley Was Formed

ALL California has been glaciated, the low plains and valleys as well as the mountains. Traces of an ice-sheet, thousands of feet in thickness, beneath whose heavy folds the present landscapes have been molded, may be found everywhere, though glaciers now exist only among the peaks of the High Sierra. No other mountain chain on this or any other of the continents that I have seen is so rich as the Sierra in bold, striking, well-preserved glacial monuments. Indeed, every feature is more or less tellingly glacial. Not a peak, ridge, dome, cañon, yosemite, lake-basin, stream or forest will you see that does not in some way explain the past existence and modes of action of flowing, grinding, sculpturing, soil-making, scenery-making ice. For, notwithstanding the post-glacial agents—the air, rain, snow, frost, river, avalanche, etc.—have been at work upon the greater portion of the Range for tens of thousands of stormy years, each engraving its own characters more and more deeply over those of the ice, the latter are so enduring and so heavily emphasized, they still rise in sublime relief, clear and legible, through every after-inscription. The landscapes of North Greenland, Antarctica, and some of those of our own Alaska, are still being fashioned beneath a slow-crawling mantle of ice, from a quarter of a mile to probably more than a mile in thickness, presenting noble illustrations of the ancient condition of California, when its sublime scenery lay hidden in process of formation. On the Himalaya, the mountains of Norway and Switzerland, the Caucasus, and on most of those of Alaska, their ice-mantle has been melted down into separate glaciers that flow river-like through the valleys, illustrating a similar past condition in the Sierra, when every cañon and valley was the channel of an ice-stream, all of which may be easily traced back to their fountains, where some sixty-five or seventy of their topmost residual branches still linger beneath protecting mountain shadows.

The change from one to another of those glacial conditions was slow as we count time. When the great cycle of snow years, called the Glacial Period, was nearly complete in California, the ice-mantle, wasting from season to season faster than it was renewed, began to withdraw from the lowlands and gradually became shallower everywhere. Then the highest of the Sierra domes and dividing ridges, containing distinct glaciers between them, began to appear above the icy sea. These first river-like glaciers remained united in one continuous sheet toward the summit of the Range for many centuries. But as the snow-fall diminished, and the climate became milder, this upper part of the ice-sheet was also in turn separated into smaller distinct glaciers, and these again into still smaller ones, while at the same time all were growing shorter and shallower, though fluctuations of the climate now and then occurred that brought their receding ends to a standstill, or even enabled them to advance for a few tens or hundreds of years.

Meanwhile, hardy, home-seeking plants and animals, after long waiting, flocked to their appointed places, pushing bravely on higher and higher, along every sun-warmed slope, closely following the retreating ice, which, like shreds of summer clouds, at length vanished from the new-born mountains, leaving them in all their main, telling features nearly as we find them now.

Tracing the ways of glaciers, learning how Nature sculptures mountain-waves in making scenery-beauty that so mysteriously influences every human being, is glorious work.

The most striking and attractive of the glacial phenomena in the upper Yosemite region are the polished glacier pavements, because they are so beautiful, and their beauty is of so rare a kind, so unlike any portion of the loose, deeply weathered lowlands where people make homes and earn their bread. They are simply flat or gently undulating areas of hard resisting granite, which present the unchanged surface upon which with enormous pressure the ancient glaciers flowed. They are found in most perfect condition in the subalpine region, at an elevation of from eight thousand to nine thousand feet. Some are miles in extent, only slightly interrupted by spots that have given way to the weather, while the best preserved portions reflect the sunbeams like calm water or glass, and shine as if polished afresh every day, notwithstanding they have been exposed to corroding rains, dew, frost, and snow measureless thousands of years.

The attention of wandering hunters and prospectors, who see so many mountain wonders, is seldom commanded by other glacial phenomena, moraines however regular and artificial-looking, cañons however deep or strangely modeled, rocks however high; but when they come to these shining pavements they stop and stare in wondering admiration, kneel again and again to examine the brightest spots, and try hard to account for their mysterious shining smoothness. They may have seen the winter avalanches of snow

The Ancient Yosemite Glaciers

descending in awful majesty through the woods, scouring the rocks and sweeping away like weeds the trees that stood in their way, but conclude that this cannot be the work of avalanches, because the scratches and fine polished striæ show that the agent, whatever it was, moved along the sides of high rocks and ridges and up over the tops of them as well as down their slopes. Neither can they see how water may possibly have been the agent, for they find the same strange polish upon ridges and domes thousands of feet above the reach of any conceivable flood. Of all the agents of whose work they know anything, only the wind seems capable of moving across the face of the country in the directions indicated by the scratches and grooves. The Indian name of Lake Tenaya is "Pyweak"—the lake of shining rocks. One of the Yosemite tribe, Indian Tom, came to me and asked if I could tell him what had made the Tenaya rocks so smooth. Even dogs and horses, when first led up the mountains, study geology to this extent that they gaze wonderingly at the strange brightness of the ground and smell it, and place their feet cautiously upon it as if afraid of falling or sinking.

In the production of this admirable hard finish, the glaciers in many places flowed with a pressure of more than a thousand tons to the square yard, planing down granite, slate, and quartz alike, and bringing out the veins and crystals of the rocks with beautiful distinctness. Over large areas below the sources of the Tuolumne and Merced the granite is porphyritic; feldspar crystals an inch or two in length in many places form the greater part of the rock, and these, when planed off level with the general surface, give rise to a beautiful mosaic on which the happy sunbeams plash and glow in passionate enthusiasm. Here lie the brightest of all the Sierra landscapes. The Range both to the north and south of this region was, perhaps, glaciated about as heavily, but because the rocks are less resisting, their polished surfaces have mostly given way to the weather, leaving only small imperfect patches. The lower remnants of the old glacial surface occur at an elevation of from 3000 to 5000 feet above the sea level, and twenty to thirty miles below the axis of the Range. The short, steeply inclined cañons of the eastern flank also contain enduring, brilliantly striated and polished rocks, but these are less magnificent than those of the broad western flank.

One of the best general views of the brightest and best of the Yosemite park landscapes that every Yosemite tourist should see, is to be had from the top of Fairview Dome, a lofty conoidal rock near Cathedral Peak that long ago I named the Tuolumne Glacier Monument, one of the most striking and best preserved of the domes. Its burnished crown is about 1500 feet above the Tuolumne Meadows and 10,000 above the sea. At first sight it seems inaccessible, though a good climber will find it may be scaled on the south side. About half-way up you will find it so steep that there is danger of slipping, but feldspar crystals, two or three inches long, of which the rock is full, having offered greater resistance to atmospheric erosion than the mass of the rock in which they are imbedded, have been brought into slight relief in some places, roughening the surface here and there, and affording helping footholds.

The summit is burnished and scored like the sides and base, the scratches and striæ indicating that the mighty Tuolumne Glacier swept over it as if it were only a mere boulder in the bottom of its channel. The pressure it withstood must have been enormous. Had it been less solidly built it would have been carried away, ground into moraine fragments, like the adjacent rock in which it lay imbedded; for, great as it is, it is only a hard residual knot like the Yosemite domes, brought into relief by the removal of less re-sisting rock about it; an illustration of the survival of the strongest and most favorably situated.

Hardly less wonderful is the resistance it has offered to the trying mountain weather since first its crown rose above the icy sea. The whole quantity of post-glacial wear and tear it has suffered has not degraded it a hundredth of an inch, as may readily be shown by the polished portions of the surface. A few erratic boulders, nicely poised on its crown, tell an interesting story. They came from the summit-peaks twelve miles away, drifting like chips on the frozen sea, and were stranded here when the top of the monu-ment merged from the ice, while their companions, whose posi-tions chanced to be above the slopes of the sides where they could not find rest, were carried farther on by falling back on the shallow-ing ice current.

The general view from the summit consists of a sublime as-semblage of ice-born rocks and mountains, long wavering ridges, meadows, lakes, and forest-covered moraines, hundreds of square miles of them. The lofty summit-peaks rise grandly along the sky to the east, the gray pillared slopes of the Hoffman Range toward the west, and a billowy sea of shining rocks like the Monument, some of them almost as high and which from their peculiar sculp-ture seem to be rolling westward in the middle ground, something like breaking waves. Immediately beneath you are the Big Tuol-umne Meadows, smooth lawns with large breadths of woods on either side, and watered by the young Tuolumne River, rushing cool and clear from its many snow- and ice-fountains. Nearly all the upper part of the basin of the Tuolumne Glacier is in sight, one

The Yosemite

of the greatest and most influential of all the Sierra ice-rivers. Lavishly flooded by many a noble affluent from the ice-laden flanks of Mounts Dana, Lyell, McClure, Gibbs, Conness, it poured its majestic outflowing current full against the end of the Hoffman Range, which divided and deflected it to right and left, just as a river of water is divided against an island in the middle of its channel. Two distinct glaciers were thus formed, one of which flowed through the great Tuolumne Cañon and Hetch Hetchy Valley, while the other swept upward in a deep current two miles wide across the divide, five hundred feet high between the basins of the Tuolumne and Merced, into the Tenaya Basin, and thence down through the Tenaya Cañon and Yosemite.

The map-like distinctness and freshness of this glacial landscape cannot fail to excite the attention of every beholder, no matter how little of its scientific significance may be recognized. These bald, westward-leaning rocks, with their rounded backs and shoulders toward the glacier fountains of the summit-mountains, and their split, angular fronts looking in the opposite direction, explain the tremendous grinding force with which the ice-flood passed over them, and also the direction of its flow. And the mountain peaks around the sides of the upper general Tuolumne Basin, with their sharp unglaciated summits and polished rounded sides, indicate the height to which the glaciers rose; while the numerous moraines, curving and swaying in beautiful lines, mark the boundaries of the main trunk and its tributaries as they existed toward the close of the glacial winter. None of the commerical highways of the land or sea, marked with buoys and lamps, fences, and guideboards, is so unmistakably indicated as are these broad, shining trails of the vanished Tuolumne Glacier and its far-reaching tributaries.

The Ancient Yosemite Glaciers

I should like now to offer some nearer views of a few characteristic specimens of these wonderful old ice-streams, though it is not easy to make a selection from so vast a system intimately interblended. The main branches of the Merced Glacier are, perhaps, best suited to our purpose, because their basins, full of telling inscriptions, are the ones most attractive and accessible to the Yosemite visitors who like to look beyond the valley walls. They number five, and may well be called Yosemite glaciers, since they were the agents Nature used in developing and fashioning the grand Valley. The names I have given them are, beginning with the northernmost, Yosemite Creek, Hoffman, Tenaya, South Lyell, and Illilouette Glaciers. These all converged in admirable poise around from northeast to southeast, welded themselves together into the main Yosemite Glacier, which, grinding gradually deeper, swept down through the Valley, receiving small tributaries on its way from the Indian, Sentinel, and Pohono Cañons; and at length flowed out of the Valley, and on down the Range in a general westerly direction. At the time that the tributaries mentioned above were well defined as to their boundaries, the upper portion of the valley walls, and the highest rocks about them, such as the Domes, the uppermost of the Three Brothers and the Sentinel, rose above the surface of the ice. But during the Valley's earlier history, all its rocks, however lofty, were buried beneath a continuous sheet, which swept on above and about them like the wind, the upper portion of the current flowing steadily, while the lower portion went mazing and swedging down in the crooked and dome-blocked cañons toward the head of the Valley.

Every glacier of the Sierra fluctuated in width and depth and length, and consequently in degree of individuality, down to the latest glacial days. It must, therefore, be borne in mind that the following description of the Yosemite glaciers applies only to their separate condition, and to that phase of their separate condition that they presented toward the close of the glacial period after most of their work was finished, and all the more telling features of the Valley and the adjacent region were brought into relief.

The comparatively level, many-fountained Yosemite Creek Glacier was about fourteen miles in length by four or five in width, and from five hundred to a thousand feet deep. Its principal tributaries, drawing their sources from the northern spurs of the Hoffman Range, at first pursued a westerly course; then, uniting with each other, and a series of short affluents from the western rim of the basin, the trunk thus formed swept around to the southward in a magnificent curve, and poured its ice over the north wall of Yosemite in cascades about two miles wide. This broad and comparatively shallow glacier formed a sort of crawling, wrinkled ice-cloud, that gradually became more regular in shape and river-like as it grew older. Encircling peaks began to overshadow its highest fountains, rock islets rose here and there amid its ebbing currents, and its picturesque banks, adorned with domes and round-backed ridges, extended in massive grandeur down to the brink of the Yosemite walls.

In the meantime the chief Hoffman tributaries, slowly receding to the shelter of the shadows covering their fountains, continued to live and work independently, spreading soil, deepening lake-basins and giving finishing touches to the sculpture in general. At length these also vanished, and the whole basin is now full of light. Forests flourish luxuriantly upon its ample moraines, lakes and meadows shine and bloom amid its polished domes, and a thousand gardens adorn the banks of its streams.

The Ancient Yosemite Glaciers

It is to the great width and even slope of the Yosemite Creek Glacier that we owe the unrivaled height and sheerness of the Yosemite Falls. For had the positions of the ice-fountains and the structure of the rocks been such as to cause down-thrusting concentration of the Glacier as it approached the Valley, then, instead of a high vertical fall we should have had a long slanting cascade, which after all would perhaps have been as beautiful and interesting, if we only had a mind to see it so.

The short, comparatively swift-flowing Hoffman Glacier, whose fountains extend along the south slopes of the Hoffman Range, offered a striking contrast to the one just described. The erosive energy of the latter was diffused over a wide field of sunken, boulder-like domes and ridges. The Hoffman Glacier, on the contrary, moved right ahead on a comparatively even surface, making a descent of nearly five thousand feet in five miles, steadily contracting and deepening its current, and finally united with the Tenaya Glacier as one of its most influential tributaries in the development and sculpture of the great Half Dome, North Dome and the rocks adjacent to them about the head of the Valley.

The story of its death is not unlike that of its companion already described, though the declivity of its channel, and its uniform exposure to sun-heat prevented any considerable portion of its current from becoming torpid, lingering only well up on the mountain slopes to finish their sculpture and encircle them with a zone of moraine soil for forests and gardens. Nowhere in all this wonderful region will you find more beautiful trees and shrubs and flowers covering the traces of ice.

The rugged Tenaya Glacier wildly crevassed here and there above the ridges it had to cross, instead of drawing its sources direct from the summit of the Range, formed, as we have seen, one of the outlets of the great Tuolumne Glacier, issuing from this noble fountain like a river from a lake, two miles wide, about fourteen miles long, and from 1500 to 2000 feet deep.

In leaving the Tuolumne region it crossed over the divide, as mentioned above, between the Tuolumne and Tenaya basins, making an ascent of five hundred feet. Hence, after contracting its wide current and receiving a strong affluent from the fountains about Cathedral Peak, it poured its massive flood over the north-eastern rim of its basin in splendid cascades. Then, crushing heavily against the Clouds' Rest Ridge, it bore down upon the Yosemite domes with concentrated energy.

Toward the end of the ice period, while its Hoffman companion continued to grind rock-meal for coming plants, the main trunk became torpid, and vanished, exposing wide areas of rolling rock-waves and glistening pavements, on whose channelless surface water ran wild and free. And because the trunk vanished almost simultaneously throughout its whole extent, no terminal moraines are found in its cañon channel; nor, since its walls are, in most places, too steeply inclined to admit of the deposition of moraine matter, do we find much of the two main laterals. The lowest of its residual glaciers lingered beneath the shadow of the Yosemite Half Dome; others along the base of Coliseum Peak above Lake Tenaya and along the precipitous wall extending from the lake to the Big Tuolumne Meadows. The latter, on account of the uniformity and continuity of their protecting shadows, formed moraines of considerable length and regularity that are liable to be mistaken for portions of the left lateral of the Tuolumne tributary glacier.

The Ancient Yosemite Glaciers

Spend all the time you can spare or steal on the tracks of this grand old glacier, charmed and enchanted by its magnificent cañon, lakes and cascades and resplendent glacier pavements.

The Nevada Glacier was longer and more symmetrical than the last, and the only one of the Merced system whose sources extended directly back to the main summits on the axis of the Range. Its numerous fountains were ranged side by side in three series, at an elevation of from 10,000 to 12,000 feet above the sea. The first, on the right side of the basin, extended from the Matterhorn to Cathedral Peak; that on the left through the Merced group, and these two parallel series were united by a third that extended around the head of the basin in a direction at right angles to the others.

The three ranges of high peaks and ridges that supplied the snow for these fountains, together with the Clouds' Rest Ridge, nearly inclose a rectangular basin, that was filled with a massive sea of ice, leaving an outlet toward the west through which flowed the main trunk glacier, three-fourths of a mile to a mile and a half wide, fifteen miles long, and from 1000 to 1500 feet deep, and entered Yosemite between the Half Dome and Mount Starr King.

Could we have visited Yosemite Valley at this period of its history, we should have found its ice cascades vastly more glorious than their tiny water representatives of the present day. One of the grandest of these was formed by that portion of the Nevada Glacier that poured over the shoulder of the Half Dome.

This glacier, as a whole, resembled an oak, with a gnarled swelling base and wide-spreading branches. Picturesque rocks of every conceivable form adorned its banks, among which glided the numerous tributaries, mottled with black and red and gray boulders, from the fountain peaks, while ever and anon, as the deliberate centuries passed away, dome after dome raised its burnished crown above the ice-flood to enrich the slowly opening landscapes.

The principal moraines occur in short irregular sections along the sides of the cañons, their fragmentary condition being due to interruptions caused by portions of the sides of the cañon walls being too steep for moraine matter to lie on, and to down-sweeping torrents and avalanches. The left lateral of the trunk may be traced about five miles from the mouth of the first main tributary to the Illilouette Cañon. The corresponding section of the right lateral, extending from Cathedral tributary to the Half Dome, is more complete because of the more favorable character of the north side of the cañon. A short side-glacier came in against it from the slopes of Clouds' Rest; but being fully exposed to the sun, it was melted long before the main trunk, allowing the latter to deposit this portion of its moraine undisturbed. Some conception of the size and appearance of this fine moraine may be gained by following the Clouds' Rest trail from Yosemite, which crosses it obliquely and conducts past several sections made by streams. Slate boulders may be seen that must have come from the Lyell group, twelve miles distant. But the bulk of the moraine is composed of porphyritic granite derived from Feldspar and Cathedral Valleys.

On the sides of the moraines we find a series of terraces, indicating fluctuations in the level of the glacier, caused by variations of snow-fall, temperature, etc., showing that the climate of the glacial period was diversified by cycles of milder or stormier seasons similar to those of post-glacial time.

After the depth of the main trunk diminished to about five

The Ancient Yosemite Glaciers

hundred feet, the greater portion became torpid, as is shown by the moraines, and lay dying in its crooked channel like a wounded snake, maintaining for a time a feeble squirming motion in places of exceptional depth, or where the bottom of the cañon was more steeply inclined. The numerous fountain-wombs, however, continued fruitful long after the trunk had vanished, giving rise to an imposing array of short residual glaciers, extending around the rim of the general basin a distance of nearly twenty-four miles. Most of these have but recently succumbed to the new climate, dying in turn as determined by elevation, size, and exposure, leaving only a few feeble survivors beneath the coolest shadows, which are now slowly completing the sculpture of one of the noblest of the Yosemite basins.

The comparatively shallow glacier that at this time filled the Illilouette Basin, though once far from shallow, more resembled a lake than a river of ice, being nearly half as wide as it was long. Its greatest length was about ten miles, and its depth perhaps nowhere much exceeded 1000 feet. Its chief fountains, ranged along the west side of the Merced group, at an elevation of about 10,000 feet, gave birth to fine tributaries that flowed in a westerly direction, and united in the center of the basin. The broad trunk at first flowed northwestward, then curved to the northward, deflected by the lofty wall forming its western bank, and finally united with the grand Yosemite trunk, opposite Glacier Point.

All the phenomena relating to glacial action in this basin are remarkably simple and orderly, on account of the sheltered positions occupied by its ice-fountains, with reference to the disturbing effects of larger glaciers from the axis of the main Range earlier in the period. From the eastern base of the Starr King cone you may obtain a fine view of the principal moraines sweeping grandly out into the middle of the basin from the shoulders of the peaks, between which the ice-fountains lay. The right lateral of the tributary, which took its rise between Red and Merced Mountains, measures two hundred and fifty feet in height at its upper extremity, and displays three well-defined terraces, similar to those of the South Lyell Glacier. The comparative smoothness of the uppermost terrace shows that it is considerably more ancient than the others, many of the boulders of which it is composed having crumbled. A few miles to the westward, this moraine has an average slope of twenty-seven degrees, and an elevation above the bottom of the channel of six hundred and sixty feet. Near the middle of the main basin, just where the regularly formed medial and lateral moraines flatten out and disappear, there is a remarkably smooth field of gravel, planted with arctostaphylos, that looks at the distance of a mile like a delightful meadow. Stream sections show the gravel deposit to be composed of the same material as the moraines, but finer, and more water-worn from the action of converging torrents issuing from the tributary glaciers after the trunk was melted. The southern boundary of the basin is a strikingly perfect wall, gray on the top, and white down the sides and at the base with snow, in which many a crystal brook takes rise. The northern boundary is made up of smooth undulating masses of gray granite, that lift here and there into beautiful domes of which the Starr King cluster is the finest, while on the east tower of the majestic fountain-peaks with wide cañons and neve amphitheaters between them, whose variegated rocks show out gloriously against the sky.

The ice-plows of this charming basin, ranged side by side in orderly gangs, furrowed the rocks with admirable uniformity, pro-

The Ancient Yosemite Glaciers

ducing irrigating channels for a brood of wild streams, and abundance of rich soil adapted to every requirement of garden and grove. No other section of the Yosemite uplands is in so perfect a state of glacial cultivation. Its domes, and peaks, and swelling rock-waves, however majestic in themselves, and yet submissively subordinate to the garden center. The other basins we have been describing are combinations of sculptured rocks, embellished with gardens and groves; the Illilouette is one grand garden and forest, embellished with rocks, each of the five beautiful in its own way, and all as harmoniously related as are the five petals of a flower. After uniting in the Yosemite Valley, and expending the down-thrusting energy derived from their combined weight and the declivity of their channels, the grand trunk flowed on through and out of the Valley. In effecting its exit a considerable ascent was made, traces of which may still be seen on the abraded rocks at the lower end of the Valley, while the direction pursued after leaving the Valley is surely indicated by the immense lateral moraines extending from the ends of the walls at an elevation of from 1500 to 1800 feet. The right lateral moraine was disturbed by a large tributary glacier that occupied the basin of Cascade Creek, causing considerable complication in its structure. The left is simple in form for several miles of its length, or to the point where a tributary came in from the southeast. But both are greatly obscured by the forests and underbrush growing upon them, and by the denuding action of rains and melting snows, etc. It is, therefore, the less to be wondered at that these moraines, made up of material derived from the distant fountain-mountains, and from the Valley itself, were not sooner recognized.

The ancient glacier systems of the Tuolumne, San Joaquin,

Kern, and Kings River Basins were developed on a still grander scale and are so replete with interest that the most sketchy outline descriptions of each, with the works they have accomplished, would fill many a volume. Therefore I can do but little more than invite everybody who is free to go and see for himself.

The action of flowing ice, whether in the form of river-like glaciers or broad mantles, especially the part it played in sculpturing the earth, is as yet but little understood. Water rivers work openly where people dwell, and so does the rain, and the sea, thundering on all the shores of the world; and the universal ocean of air, though invisible, speaks aloud in a thousand voices, and explains its modes of working and its power. But glaciers, back in their white solitudes, work apart from men, exerting their tremendous energies in silence and darkness. Outspread, spirit-like, they brood above the predestined landscapes, work on unwearied through immeasurable ages, until, in the fullness of time, the mountains and valleys are brought forth, channels furrowed for rivers, basins made for lakes and meadows, and arms of the sea, soils spread for forests and fields; then they shrink and vanish like summer clouds.

12

How Best to Spend One's Yosemite Time

ONE-DAY EXCURSIONS
No. 1.

IF I were so time-poor as to have only one day to spend in Yosemite I should start at daybreak, say at three o'clock in midsummer, with a pocketful of any sort of dry breakfast stuff, for Glacier Point, Sentinel Dome, the head of Illilouette Fall, Nevada Fall, the top of Liberty Cap, Vernal Fall and the wild boulder-choked River Cañon. The trail leaves the Valley at the base of the Sentinel Rock, and as you slowly saunter from point to point along its many accommodating zigzags nearly all the Valley rocks and falls arc seen in striking, ever-changing combinations. At an elevation of about five hundred feet a particularly fine, wide-sweeping view down the Valley is obtained, past the sheer face of the Sentinel and between the Cathedral Rocks and El Capitan. At a height of about 1500 feet the great Half Dome comes full in sight, overshadowing every other feature of the Valley to the eastward. From Glacier Point you look down 3000 feet over the edge of its sheer face to the meadows and groves and innumerable yellow pine spires, with the meandering river sparkling and spangling through the midst of them. Across the Valley a great telling view is presented of the Royal Arches,

The Yosemite

North Dome, Indian Cañon, Three Brothers and El Capitan, with the dome-paved basin of Yosemite Creek and Mount Hoffman in the background. To the eastward, the Half Dome close beside you looking higher and more wonderful than ever; southeastward the Starr King, girdled with silver firs, and the spacious garden-like basin of the Illilouette and its deeply sculptured fountain-peaks, called "The Merced Group"; and beyond all, marshaled along the eastern horizon, the icy summits on the axis of the Range and broad swaths of forests growing on ancient moraines, while the Nevada, Vernal and Yosemite Falls are not only full in sight but are distinctly heard as if one were standing beside them in their spray.

The views from the summit of Sentinel Dome are still more extensive and telling. Eastward the crowds of peaks at the head of the Merced, Tuolumne and San Joaquin Rivers are presented in bewildering array; westward, the vast forests, yellow foothills and the broad San Joaquin plains and the Coast Ranges, hazy and dim in the distance.

From Glacier Point go down the trail into the lower end of the Illilouette basin, cross Illilouette Creek and follow it to the Fall where from an outjutting rock at its head you will get a fine view of its rejoicing waters and wild cañon and the Half Dome. Thence returning to the trail, follow it to the head of the Nevada Fall. Linger here an hour or two, for not only have you glorious views of the wonderful fall, but of its wild, leaping, exulting rapids and, greater than all, the stupendous scenery into the heart of which the white passionate river goes wildly thundering, surpassing everything of its kind in the world. After an unmeasured hour or so of this glory, all your body aglow, nerve currents flashing through you never before felt, go to the top of the Liberty Cap, only a glad saunter now that your legs as well as head and heart are awake and rejoicing with everything. The Liberty Cap, a companion of the Half Dome, is sheer and inaccessible on three of its sides but on the east a gentle, ice-burnished, juniper-dotted slope extends to the summit where other wonderful views are displayed where all are wonderful: the south side and shoulders of Half Dome and Clouds' Rest, the beautiful Little Yosemite Valley and its many domes, the Starr King cluster of domes, Sentinel Dome, Glacier Point, and, perhaps the most tremendously impressive of all, the views of the hopper-shaped cañon of the river from the head of the Nevada Fall to the head of the Valley.

Returning to the trail you descend between the Nevada Fall and the Liberty Cap with fine side views of both the fall and the rock, pass on through clouds of spray and along the rapids to the head of the Vernal Fall, about a mile below the Nevada. Linger here if night is still distant, for views of this favorite fall and the stupendous rock scenery about it. Then descend a stairway by its side, follow a dim trail through its spray, and a plain one along the border of the boulder-dashed rapids and so back to the wide, tranquil Valley.

ONE-DAY EXCURSIONS
No. 2.

Another grand one-day excursion is to the Upper Yosemite Fall, the top of the highest of the Three Brothers, called Eagle Peak on the Geological Survey maps; the brow of El Capitan; the head of the Ribbon Fall; across the beautiful Ribbon Creek Basin; and back to the Valley by the Big Oak Flat wagon-road.

[147]

The Yosemite

The trail leaves the Valley on the east side of the largest of the earthquake taluses immediately opposite the Sentinel Rock and as it passes within a few rods of the foot of the great fall, magnificent views are obtained as you approach it and pass through its spray, though when the snow is melting fast you will be well drenched. From the foot of the Fall the trail zigzags up a narrow cañon between the fall and a plain mural cliff that is burnished here and there by glacial action.

You should stop a while on a flat iron-fenced rock a little below the head of the fall beside the enthusiastic throng of starry comet-like waters to learn something of their strength, their marvelous variety of forms, and above all, their glorious music, gathered and composed from the snow-storms, hail-, rain- and wind-storms that have fallen on their glacier-sculptured, domey, ridgy basin. Refreshed and exhilarated, you follow your trail-way through silver fir and pine woods to Eagle Peak, where the most comprehensive of all the views to be had on the north-wall heights are displayed. After an hour or two of gazing, dreaming, studying the tremendous topography, etc., trace the rim of the Valley to the grand El Capitan ridge and go down to its brow, where you will gain everlasting impressions of Nature's steadfastness and power combined with ineffable fineness of beauty.

Dragging yourself away, go to the head of the Ribbon Fall, thence across the beautiful Ribbon Creek Basin to the Big Oak Flat stage-road, and down its fine grades to the Valley, enjoying glorious Yosemite scenery all the way to the foot of El Capitan and your camp.

How Best to Spend One's Yosemite Time

TWO-DAY EXCURSIONS
No. 1

For a two-day trip I would go straight to Mount Hoffman, spend the night on the summit, next morning go down by May Lake to Tenaya Lake and return to the Valley by Cloud's Rest and the Nevada and Vernal Falls. As on the foregoing excursion, you leave the Valley by the Yosemite Falls trail and follow it to the Tioga wagon-road, a short distance east of Porcupine Flat. From that point push straight up to the summit. Mount Hoffman is a mass of gray granite that rises almost in the center of the Yosemite Park, about eight or ten miles in a straight line from the Valley. Its southern slopes are low and easily climbed, and adorned here and there with castle-like crumbling piles and long jagged crests that look like artificial masonry; but on the north side it is abruptly precipitous and banked with lasting snow. Most of the broad summit is comparatively level and thick sown with crystals, quartz, mica, hornblende, feldspar, granite, zircon, tourmaline, etc., weathered out and strewn closely and loosely as if they had been sown broadcast. Their radiance is fairly dazzling in sunlight, almost hiding the multitude of small flowers that grow among them. At first sight only these radiant crystals are likely to be noticed, but looking closely you discover a multitude of very small gilias, phloxes, mimulus, etc., many of them with more petals than leaves. On the borders of little streams larger plants flourish—lupines, daisies, asters, goldenrods, hairbell, mountain columbine, potentilla, astragalus and a few gentians; with charming heathworts—bryanthus, cassiope, kalmia, vaccinium in boulder-fringing rings or bank covers. You saunter among the crystals and flowers as if you were walking among stars. From the summit nearly all the Yosemite Park is displayed like a map: forests, lakes, meadows, and snowy peaks. Northward lies Yosemite's wide basin with its domes and small lakes, shining like larger crystals; eastward the rocky, meadowy Tuolumne region, bounded by its snowy peaks in glorious array; southward Yosemite and westward the vast forest. On no other Yosemite Park mountain are you more likely to linger. You will find it a magnificent sky camp. Clumps of dwarf pine and mountain hemlock will furnish resin roots and branches for fuel and light, and the rills, sparkling water. Thousands of the little plant people will gaze at your camp-fire with the crystals and stars, companions and guardians as you lie at rest in the heart of the vast serene night.

The most telling of all the wide Hoffman views is the basin of the Tuolumne with its meadows, forests and hundreds of smooth rock-waves that appear to be coming rolling on towards you like high heaving waves ready to break, and beyond these the great mountains. But best of all are the dawn and the sunrise. No mountain top could be better placed for this most glorious of mountain views—to watch and see the deepening colors of the dawn and the sunbeams streaming through the snowy High Sierra passes, awakening the lakes and crystals, the chilled plant people and winged people, and making everything shine and sing in pure glory.

With your heart aglow, spangling Lake Tenaya and Lake May will beckon you away for walks on their ice-burnished shores. Leave Tenaya at the west end, cross to the south side of the outlet, and gradually work your way up in an almost straight south direction to the summit of the divide between Tenaya Creek and the main upper Merced River or Nevada Creek and follow the divide to Clouds' Rest. After a glorious view from the crest of this lofty granite wave you will find a trail on its western end that will lead you down past Nevada and Vernal Falls to the Valley in good time, provided you left your Hoffman sky camp early.

TWO-DAY EXCURSIONS
No. 2.

Another grand two-day excursion is the same as the first of the one-day trips, as far as the head of Illilouette Fall. From there trace the beautiful stream up through the heart of its magnificent forests and gardens to the cañons between the Red and Merced Peaks, and pass the night where I camped forty-one years ago. Early next morning visit the small glacier on the north side of Merced Peak, the first of the sixty-five that I discovered in the Sierra.

Glacial phenomena in the Illilouette Basin are on the grandest scale, and in the course of my explorations I found that the cañon and moraines between the Merced and Red Mountains were the most interesting of them all. The path of the vanished glacier shone in many places as if washed with silver, and pushing up the cañon on this bright road I passed lake after lake in solid basins of granite and many a meadow along the cañon stream that links them together. The main lateral moraines that bound the view below the cañon are from a hundred to nearly two hundred feet high and wonderfully regular, like artificial embankments, covered with a magnificent growth of silver fir and pine. But this garden and forest luxuriance is speedily left behind, and patches of bryanthus, cassiope and arctic willows begin to appear. The small lakes which a few miles down the Valley are so richly bordered with flowery meadows have at an elevation of 10,000 feet only small brown mats of carex, leaving bare rocks around more than half their shores. Yet, strange to say, amid all this arctic repression the mountain pine on ledges and buttresses of Red Mountain seems to find the climate best suited to it. Some specimens that I measured were over a hundred feet high and twenty-four feet in circumference, showing hardly a trace of severe storms, looking as fresh and vigorous as the giants of the lower zones. Evening came on just as I got fairly into the main cañon. It is about a mile wide and a little less than two miles long. The crumbling spurs of Red Mountain bound it on the north, the somber cliffs of Merced Mountain on the south and a deeply-serrated, splintered ridge curving around from mountain to mountain shuts it in on the east. My camp was on the brink of one of the lakes in a thicket of mountain hemlock, partly sheltered from the wind. Early next morning I set out to trace the ancient glacier to its head. Passing around the north shore of my camp lake I followed the main stream from one lakelet to another. The dwarf pines and hemlocks disappeared and the stream was bordered with icicles. The main lateral moraines that extend from the mouth of the cañon are continued in straggling masses along the walls. Tracing the streams back to the highest of its little lakes, I noticed a deposit of fine gray mud, something like the mud worn from a grindstone. This suggested its glacial origin, for the stream that was carrying it issued from a raw-looking moraine that seemed to be in process of formation. It is from sixty to over a hundred feet high in front, with a slope of about thirty-eight degrees. Climbing to the top of it, I discovered a very small but well-characterized glacier swooping down from the shadowy cliffs of the mountain to its terminal moraine. The ice appeared on all the lower portion of the glacier; farther up it was covered with snow.

How Best to Spend One's Yosemite Time

The uppermost crevasse or "bergeschrund" was from twelve to fourteen feet wide. The melting snow and ice formed a network of rills that ran gracefully down the surface of the glacier, merrily singing in their shining channels. After this discovery I made excursions over all the High Sierra and discovered that what at first sight looked like snowfields were in great part glaciers which were completing the sculpture of the summit peaks.

Rising early,—which will be easy, as your bed will be rather cold and you will not be able to sleep much anyhow,—after visiting the glacier, climb the Red Mountain and enjoy the magnificent views from the summit. I counted forty lakes from one standpoint on this mountain, and the views to the westward over the Illilouette Basin, the most superbly forested of all the basins whose waters drain into Yosemite, and those of the Yosemite rocks, especially the Half Dome and the upper part of the north wall, are very fine. But, of course, far the most imposing view is the vast array of snowy peaks along the axis of the Range. Then from the top of this peak, light and free and exhilarated with mountain air and mountain beauty, you should run lightly down the northern slope of the mountain, descend the cañon between Red and Gray Mountains, thence northward along the bases of Gray Mountain and Mount Clark and go down into the head of Little Yosemite, and thence down past the Nevada and Vernal Falls to the Valley, a truly glorious two-day trip!

A THREE-DAY EXCURSION

The best three-day excursion, as far as I can see, is the same as the first of the two-day trips until you reach Lake Tenaya. There instead of returning to the Valley, follow the Tioga road around the northwest side of the lake, over to the Tuolumne Meadows and up to the west base of Mount Dana. Leave the road there and make straight for the highest point on the timber line between Mounts Dana and Gibbs and camp there.

On the morning of the third day go to the top of Mount Dana in time for the glory of the dawn and the sunrise over the gray Mono Desert and the sublime forest of High Sierra peaks. When you leave the mountain go far enough down the north side for a view of the Dana Glacier, then make your way back to the Tioga road, follow it along the Tuolumne Meadows to the crossing of Budd Creek where you will find the Sunrise trail branching off up the mountain-side through the forest in a southwesterly direction past the west side of Cathedral Peak, which will lead you down to the Valley by the Vernal and Nevada Falls. If you are a good walker you can leave the trail where it begins to descend a steep slope in the silver fir woods, and bear off to the right and make straight for the top of Clouds' Rest. The walking is good and almost level and from the west end of Clouds' Rest take the Clouds' Rest trail which will lead direct to the Valley by the Nevada and Vernal Falls. To any one not desperately time-poor this trip should have four days instead of three; camping the second night at the Soda Springs; thence to Mount Dana and return to the Soda Springs, camping the third night there; thence by the Sunrise trail to Cathedral Peak, visiting the beautiful Cathedral lake which lies about a mile to the west of Cathedral Peak, eating your luncheon, and thence to Clouds' Rest and the Valley as above. This is one of the most interesting of all the comparatively short trips that can be made in the whole Yosemite region. Not only do you see all the grandest of the Yosemite rocks and waterfalls and the High Sierra with their glaciers, glacier lakes and glacier meadows, etc., but sections of the magnificent silver fir, two-leaved pine, and dwarf pine zones; with the principal alpine flowers and shrubs, especially sods of dwarf vaccinium covered with flowers and fruit though less than an inch high, broad mats of dwarf willow scarce an inch high with catkins that rise straight from the ground, and glorious beds of blue gentians,—grandeur enough and beauty enough for a lifetime.

THE UPPER TUOLUMNE EXCURSION

We come now to the grandest of all the Yosemite excursions, one that requires at least two or three weeks. The best time to make it is from about the middle of July. The visitor entering the Yosemite in July has the advantage of seeing the falls not, perhaps, in their very flood prime but next thing to it; while the glacier-meadows will be in their glory and the snow on the mountains will be firm enough to make climbing safe. Long ago I made these Sierra trips, carrying only a sackful of bread with a little tea and sugar and was thus independent and free, but now that trails or carriage roads lead out of the Valley in almost every direction it is easy to take a pack animal, so that the luxury of a blanket and a supply of food can easily be had.

The best way to leave the Valley will be by the Yosemite Fall trail, camping the first night on the Tioga road opposite the east end of the Hoffman Range. Next morning climb Mount Hoffman; thence push on past Tenaya Lake into the Tuolumne Meadows and establish a central camp near the Soda Springs, from which glorious excursions can be made at your leisure. For here in this upper Tuolumne Valley is the widest, smoothest, most serenely spacious, and in every way the most delightful summer pleasure-park in all the High Sierra. And since it is connected with Yosemite by two good trails, and a fairly good carriage road that passes between Yosemite and Mount Hoffman, it is also the most accessible. It is in the heart of the High Sierra east of Yosemite, 8500 to 9000 feet above the level of the sea. The gray, picturesque Cathedral Range bounds it on the south; a similar range or spur, the highest peak of which is Mount Conness, on the north; the noble Mounts Dana, Gibbs, Mammoth, Lyell, McClure and others on the axis of the Range on the east; a heaving, billowing crowd of glacier-polished rocks and Mount Hoffman on the west. Down through the open sunny meadow-levels of the Valley flows the Tuolumne River, fresh and cool from its many glacial fountains, the highest of which are the glaciers that lie on the north sides of Mount Lyell and Mount McClure.

Along the river a series of beautiful glacier-meadows extend with but little interruption, from the lower end of the Valley to its head, a distance of about twelve miles, forming charming sauntering-grounds from which the glorious mountains may be enjoyed as they look down in divine serenity over the dark forests that clothe their bases. Narrow strips of pine woods cross the meadow-carpet from side to side, and it is somewhat roughened here and there by moraine boulders and dead trees brought down from the heights by snow avalanches; but for miles and miles it is so smooth and level that a hundred horsemen may ride abreast over it.

The main lower portion of the meadows is about four miles long and from a quarter to half a mile wide, but the width of the Valley is, on an average, about eight miles. Tracing the river, we find that it forks a mile above the Soda Springs, the main fork turning southward to Mount Lyell, the other eastward to Mount Dana and Mount Gibbs. Along both forks strips of meadow extend almost to their heads. The most beautiful portions of the meadows are spread over lake basins, which have been filled up by deposits from the river. A few of these river-lakes still exist, but they are now shallow and are rapidly approaching extinction. The sod in most places is exceedingly fine and silky and free from weeds and bushes; while charming flowers abound, especially gentians, dwarf daisies, potentillas, and the pink bells of dwarf vaccinium. On the banks of the river and its tributaries cassiope and bryanthus may be found, where the sod curls over stream banks and around boulders. The principal grass of these meadows is a delicate calamagrostis with very slender filiform leaves, and when it is in flower the ground seems to be covered with a faint purple mist, the stems of the panicles being so fine that they are almost invisible, and offer no appreciable resistance in walking through them. Along the edges of the meadows beneath the pines and throughout the greater part of the Valley tall ribbon-leaved grasses grow in abundance, chiefly bromus, triticum and agrostis.

In October the nights are frosty, and then the meadows at sunrise, when every leaf is laden with crystals, are a fine sight. The days are still warm and calm, and bees and butterflies continue to waver and hum about the late-blooming flowers until the coming of the snow, usually in November. Storm then follows storm in quick succession, burying the meadows to a depth of from ten to twenty feet, while magnificent avalanches descend through the forests from the laden heights, depositing huge piles of snow mixed with uprooted trees and boulders. In the open sunshine the snow usually lasts until the end of June but the new season's vegetation is not generally in bloom until late in July. Perhaps the best all round excursion-time after winters of average snowfall is from the middle of July to the middle or end of August. The snow is then melted from the woods and southern slopes of the mountains and the meadows and gardens are in their glory, while the weather is mostly all-reviving, exhilarating sunshine. The few clouds that rise now and then and the showers they yield are only enough to keep everything fresh and fragrant.

The groves about the Soda Springs are favorite camping-grounds on account of the cold, pleasant-tasting water charged with carbonic acid, and because of the views of the mountains across the meadow—the Glacier Monument, Cathedral Peak, Cathedral Spires, Unicorn Peak and a series of ornamental nameless companions, rising in striking forms and nearness above a dense forest growing on the left lateral moraine of the ancient Tuolumne Glacier, which, broad, deep, and far-reaching, exerted vast influence on the scenery of this portion of the Sierra. But there are fine camping-grounds all along the meadows, and one may move from grove to grove every day all summer, enjoying new homes and new beauty to satisfy every roving desire for change.

There are five main capital excursions to be made from here—to the summits of Mounts Dana, Lyell and Conness, and through the Bloody Cañon Pass to Mono Lake and the volcanoes, and down the Tuolumne Cañon, at least as far as the foot of the wonderful series of river cataracts. All of these excursions are sure to be made memorable with joyful health-giving experiences; but perhaps none of them will be remembered with keener delight than the days spent in sauntering on the broad velvet lawns by the river, sharing the sky with the mountains and trees, gaining something of their strength and peace.

The excursion to the top of Mount Dana is a very easy one; for though the mountain is 13,000 feet high, the ascent from the west side is so gentle and smooth that one may ride a mule to the very summit. Across many a busy stream, from meadow to meadow, lies your flowery way; mountains all about you, few of them hidden by irregular foregrounds. Gradually ascending, other mountains come in sight, peak rising above peak with their snow and ice in endless variety of grouping and sculpture. Now your attention is turned to the moraines, sweeping in beautiful curves from the hollows and cañons, now to the granite waves and pavements rising here and there above the heathy sod, polished a thousand years ago and still shining. Towards the base of the mountain you note the dwarfing of the trees, until at a height of about 11,000 feet you find patches of the tough, white-barked pine, pressed so flat by the ten or twenty feet of snow piled upon them every winter for centuries that you may walk over them as if walking on a shaggy rug. And, if curious about such things, you may discover specimens of this hardy tree-mountaineer not more than four feet high and about as many inches in diameter at the ground, that are from two hundred to four hundred years old, still holding bravely to life, making the most of their slender summers, shaking their tasseled needles in the breeze right cheerily, drinking the thin sunshine and maturing their fine purple cones as if they meant to live forever. The general view from the summit is one of the most extensive and sublime to be found in all the Range. To the eastward you gaze far out over the desert plains and mountains of the "Great Basin," range beyond range extending with soft outlines, blue and purple in the distance. More than six thousand feet below you lies Lake Mono, ten miles in diameter from north to south, and fourteen from west to east, lying bare in the treeless desert like a disk of burnished metal, though at times it is swept by mountain storm-winds and streaked with foam. To the southward there is a well-defined range of pale-gray extinct volcanoes, and though the highest of them rises nearly two thousand feet above the lake, you can look down from here into their circular, cup-like craters, from which a comparatively short time ago ashes and cinders were showered over the surrounding sage plains and glacier-laden mountains.

To the westward the landscape is made up of exceedingly strong, gray, glaciated domes and ridge waves, most of them comparatively low, but the largest high enough to be called mountains; separated by cañons and darkened with lines and fields of forest, Cathedral Peak and Mount Hoffman in the distance; small lakes and innumerable meadows in the foreground. Northward and southward the great snowy mountains, marshaled along the axis of the Range, are seen in all their glory, crowded together in some places like trees in groves, making landscapes of wild, extravagant, bewildering magnificence, yet calm and silent as the sky.

Some eight glaciers are in sight. One of these is the Dana Glacier on the north side of the mountain, lying at the foot of a precipice about a thousand feet high, with a lovely pale-green lake a little below it. This is one of the many, small, shrunken remnants of the vast glacial system of the Sierra that once filled the hollows and valleys of the mountains and covered all the lower ridges below the immediate summit-fountains, flowing to right and left away from the axis of the Range, lavishly fed by the snows of the glacial period.

How Best to Spend One's Yosemite Time

In the excursion to Mount Lyell the immediate base of the mountain is easily reached on meadow walks along the river. Turning to the southward above the forks of the river, you enter the narrow Lyell branch of the Valley, narrow enough and deep enough to be called a cañon. It is about eight miles long and from 2000 to 3000 feet deep. The flat meadow bottom is from about three hundred to two hundred yards wide, with gently curved margins about fifty yards wide from which rise the simple massive walls of gray granite at an angle of about thirty-three degrees, mostly timbered with a light growth of pine and streaked in many places with avalanche channels. Towards the upper end of the cañon the Sierra crown comes in sight, forming a finely balanced picture framed by the massive cañon walls. In the foreground, when the grass is in flower, you have the purple meadow willow-thickets on the river banks; in the middle distance huge swelling bosses of granite that form the base of the general mass of the mountain, with fringing lines of dark woods marking the lower curves, smoothly snow-clad except in the autumn.

If you wish to spend two days on the Lyell trip you will find a good camp-ground on the east side of the river, about a mile above a fine cascade that comes down over the cañon wall in telling style and makes good camp music. From here to the top of the mountains is usually an easy day's work. At one place near the summit careful climbing is necessary, but it is not so dangerous or difficult as to deter any one of ordinary skill, while the views are glorious. To the northward are Mammoth Mountain, Mounts Gibbs, Dana, Warren, Conness and others, unnumbered and unnamed; to the southeast the indescribably wild and jagged range of Mount Ritter and the Minarets; southwestward stretches the dividing ridge between the north fork of the San Joaquin and the Merced, uniting with the Obelisk or Merced group of peaks that form the main fountains of the Illilouette branch of the Merced; and to the north-westward extends the Cathedral spur. These spurs like distinct ranges meet at your feet; therefore you look at them mostly in the direction of their extension, and their peaks seem to be massed and crowded against one another, while immense amphitheaters, ca-ñons and subordinate ridges with their wealth of lakes, glaciers, and snow-fields, maze and cluster between them. In making the ascent in June or October the glacier is easily crossed, for then its snow mantle is smooth or mostly melted off. But in midsummer the climbing is exceedingly tedious because the snow is then weathered into curious and beautiful blades, sharp and slender, and set on edge in a leaning position. They lean towards the head of the glacier and extend across from side to side in regular order in a direction at right angles to the direction of greatest declivity, the distance between the crests being about two or three feet, and the depth of the troughs between them about three feet. A more inter-esting problem than a walk over a glacier thus sculptured and adorned is seldom presented to the mountaineer.

The Lyell Glacier is about a mile wide and less than a mile long, but presents, nevertheless, all the essential characters of large, river-like glaciers—moraines, earth-bands, blue veins, cre-vasses, etc., while the streams that issue from it are, of course, turbid with rock-mud, showing its grinding action on its bed. And it is all the more interesting since it is the highest and most endur-ing remnant of the great Tuolumne Glacier, whose traces are still distinct fifty miles away, and whose influence on the landscape was so profound. The McClure Glacier, once a tributary of the Lyell, is smaller. Thirty-eight years ago I set a series of stakes in it to determine its rate of motion. Towards the end of summer in the middle of the glacier it was only a little over an inch in twenty-four hours.

The trip to Mono from the Soda Springs can be made in a day, but many days may profitably be spent near the shores of the lake, out on its islands and about the volcanoes.

In making the trip down the Big Tuolumne Cañon, animals may be led as far as a small, grassy, forested lake-basin that lies below the crossing of the Virginia Creek trail. And from this point any one accustomed to walking on earthquake boulders, carpeted with cañon chaparral, can easily go down as far as the big cascades and return to camp in one day. Many, however, are not able to do this, and it is better to go leisurely, prepared to camp anywhere, and enjoy the marvelous grandeur of the place.

The cañon begins near the lower end of the meadows and extends to the Hetch Hetchy Valley, a distance of about eighteen miles, though it will seem much longer to any one who scrambles through it. It is from twelve hundred to about five thousand feet deep, and is comparatively narrow, but there are several roomy, park-like openings in it, and throughout its whole extent Yosemite features are displayed on a grand scale—domes, El Capitan rocks, gables, Sentinels, Royal Arches, Glacier Points, Cathedral Spires, etc. There is even a Half Dome among its wealth of rock forms, though far less sublime than the Yosemite Half Dome. Its falls and cascades are innumerable. The sheer falls, except when the snow is melting in early spring, are quite small in volume as compared with those of Yosemite and Hetch Hetchy; though in any other country many of them would be regarded as wonders. But it is the cascades or sloping falls on the main river that are the crowning glory of the cañon, and these in volume, extent and variety surpass those of any other cañon in the Sierra. The most showy and interesting of them are mostly in the upper part of the cañon, above the point of entrance of Cathedral Creek and Hoffman Creek. For miles the river is one wild, exulting, on-rushing mass of snowy purple bloom, spreading over glacial waves of granite without any definite channel, gliding in magnificent silver plumes, dashing and foaming through huge boulder-dams, leaping high into the air in wheel-like whirls, displaying glorious enthusiasm, tossing from side to side, doubling, glinting, singing in exuberance of mountain energy.

Every one who is anything of a mountaineer should go on through the entire length of the cañon, coming out by Hetch Hetchy. There is not a dull step all the way. With wide variations, it is a Yosemite Valley from end to end.

Besides these main, far-reaching, much-seeing excursions from the main central camp, there are numberless, lovely little saunters and scrambles and a dozen or so not so very little. Among the best of these are to Lambert and Fair View Domes; to the topmost spires of Cathedral Peak, and to those of the North Church, around the base of which you pass on your way to Mount Conness; to one of the very loveliest of the glacier-meadows imbedded in the pine woods about three miles north of the Soda Springs, where forty-two years ago I spent six weeks. It trends east and west, and you can find it easily by going past the base of Lambert's Dome to Dog Lake and thence up northward through the woods about a mile or so; to the shining rock-waves full of ice-burnished, feldspar crystals at the foot of the meadows; to Lake Tenaya; and, last but not least, a rather long and very hearty scramble down by the end of the meadow along the Tioga road toward Lake Tenaya to the crossing of Cathedral Creek, where you turn off and trace the creek down to its confluence with the Tuolumne. This is a genuine scramble much of the way but one of the most wonderfully telling in its glacial rock-forms and inscriptions.

If you stop and fish at every tempting lake and stream you come to, a whole month, or even two months, will not be too long for this grand High Sierra excursion. My own Sierra trip was ten years long.

OTHER TRIPS FROM THE VALLEY

Short carriage trips are usually made in the early morning to Mirror Lake to see its wonderful reflections of the Half Dome and Mount Watkins; and in the afternoon many ride down the Valley to see the Bridal Veil rainbows or up the river cañon to see those of the Vernal Fall; where, standing in the spray, not minding getting drenched, you may see what are called round rainbows, when the two ends of the ordinary bow are lengthened and meet at your feet, forming a complete circle which is broken and united again and again as determined by the varying wafts of spray. A few ambitious scramblers climb to the top of the Sentinel Rock, others walk or ride down the Valley and up to the once-famous Inspiration Point for a last grand view; while a good many appreciative tourists, who have only day or two, do no climbing or riding but spend their time sauntering on the meadows by the river, watching the falls, and the play of light and shade among the rocks from morning to night, perhaps gaining more than those who make haste up the trails in large noisy parties. Those who have unlimited time find something worth while all the year round on every accessible part of the vast, deeply sculptured walls. At least so I have found it after making the Valley my home for years.

Here are a few specimens selected from my own short trips which walkers may find useful.

One, up the river cañon, across the bridge between the Vernal and Nevada Falls, through chaparral beds and boulders to the shoulder of Half Dome, along the top of the shoulder to the dome itself, down by a crumbling slot gully and close along the base of the tremendous split front (the most awfully impressive, sheer, precipice view I ever found in all my cañon wanderings), thence up the east shoulder and along the ridge to Clouds' Rest—a glorious sunset—then a grand starry run back home to my cabin; down through the junipers, down through the firs, now in black shadows, now in white light, past roaring Nevada and Vernal, glowering ghost-like beneath their huge frowning cliffs; down the dark, gloomy cañon, through the pines of the Valley, dreamily murmuring in their calm, breezy sleep—a fine wild little excursion for good legs and good eyes—so much sun-, moon- and star-shine in it, and sublime, up-and-down rhythmical, glacial topography.

Another, to the head of Yosemite Fall by Indian Cañon; thence up the Yosemite Creek, tracing it all the way to its highest sources back of Mount Hoffman, then a wide sweep around the head of its dome-paved basin, passing its many little lakes and bogs, gardens and groves, trilling, warbling rills, and back by the Fall Cañon. This was one of my Sabbath walk, run-and-slide excursions long ago before any trail had been made on the north side of the Valley.

Another fine trip was up, bright and early, by Avalanche Ca-

How Best to Spend One's Yosemite Time

ñon to Glacier Point, along the rugged south wall, tracing all its far outs and ins to the head of the Bridal Veil Fall, thence back home, bright and late, by a brushy, bouldery slope between Cathedral rocks and Cathedral spires and along the level Valley floor. This was one of my long, bright-day and bright-night walks thirty or forty years ago when, like river and ocean currents, time flowed undivided, uncounted—a fine free, sauntery, scrambly, botanical, beauty-filled ramble. The walk up the Valley was made glorious by the marvelous brightness of the morning star. So great was her light, she made every tree cast a well-defined shadow on the smooth sandy ground.

Everybody who visits Yosemite wants to see the famous Big Trees. Before the railroad was constructed, all three of the stage-roads that entered the Valley passed through a grove of these trees by the way; namely, the Tuolumne, Merced and Mariposa groves. The Tuolumne grove was passed on the Big Oak Flat road, the Merced grove by the Coulterville road and the Mariposa grove by the Raymond and Wawona road. Now, to see any one of these groves, a special trip has to be made. Most visitors go to the Mariposa grove, the largest of the three. On this Sequoia trip you see not only the giant Big Trees but magnificent forests of silver fir, sugar pine, yellow pine, libocedrus and Douglas spruce. The trip need not require more than two days, spending a night in a good hotel at Wawona, a beautiful place on the south fork of the Merced River, and returning to the Valley or to El Portal, the terminus of the railroad. This extra trip by stage costs fifteen dollars. All the High Sierra excursions that I have sketched cost from a dollar a week to anything you like. None of mine when I was exploring the Sierra cost over a dollar a week, most of them less.

The Yosemite

EARLY HISTORY OF THE VALLEY

In the wild gold years of 1849 and '50, the Indian tribes along the western Sierra foothills became alarmed at the sudden invasion of their acorn orchard and game fields by miners, and soon began to make war upon them, in their usual murdering, plundering style. This continued until the United States Indian Commissioners succeeded in gathering them into reservations, some peacefully, others by burning their villages and stores of food. The Yosemite or Grizzly Bear tribe, fancying themselves secure in their deep mountain stronghold, were the most troublesome and defiant of all, and it was while the Mariposa battalion, under command of Major Savage, was trying to capture this warlike tribe and conduct them to the Fresno reservation that their deep mountain home, the Yosemite Valley, was discovered. From a camp on the south fork of the Merced, Major Savage sent Indian runners to the bands who were supposed to be hiding in the mountains, instructing them to tell the Indians that if they would come in and make treaty with the Commissioners they would be furnished with food and clothing and be protected, but if they did not come in he would make war upon them and kill them all. None of the Yosemite Indians responded to this general message, but when a special messenger was sent to the chief he appeared the next day. He came entirely alone and stood in dignified silence before one of the guards until invited to enter the camp. He was recognized by one of the friendly Indians as Tenaya, the old chief of the Grizzlies, and, after he had been supplied with food, Major Savage, with the aid of Indian interpreters, informed him of the wishes of the Commissioners. But the old chief was very suspicious of Savage and feared that he was taking this method of getting the tribe into his power for the purpose of revenging his personal wrong. Savage told him if he would go to the Commissioners and make peace with them as the other tribes had done there would be no more war. Tenaya inquired what was the object of taking all the Indians to the San Joaquin plain. "My people," said he, "do not want anything from the Great Father you tell me about. The Great Spirit is our father and he has always supplied us with all we need. We do not want anything from white men. Our women are able to do our work. Go, then. Let us remain in the mountains where we were born, where the ashes of our fathers have been given to the wind. I have said enough."

To this the Major answered abruptly in Indian style: "If you and your people have all you desire, why do you steal our horses and mules? Why do you rob the miners' camps? Why do you murder the white men and plunder and burn their houses?"

Tenaya was silent for some time. He evidently understood what the Major had said, for he replied, "My young men have sometimes taken horses and mules from the whites. This was wrong. It is not wrong to take the property of enemies who have wronged my people. My young men believed that the gold diggers were our enemies. We now know they are not and we shall be glad to live in peace with them. We will stay here and be friends. My people do not want to go to the plains. Some of the tribes who have gone there are very bad. We cannot live with them. Here we can defend ourselves."

To the Major Savage firmly said, "Your people must go to the Commissioners. If they do not your young men will again steal horses and kill and plunder the whites. It was your people who robbed my stores, burned my houses and murdered my men. If they do not make a treaty, your whole tribe will be destroyed. Not one of them will be left alive."

To this the old chief replied, "It is useless to talk to you about who destroyed your property and killed your people. I am old and you can kill me if you will, but it is useless to lie to you who know more than all the Indians. Therefore I will not lie to you but if you will let me return to my people I will bring them in." He was allowed to go. The next day he came back and said his people were on the way to our camp to go with the men sent by the Great Father, who was so good and rich.

Another day passed but no Indians from the deep Valley appeared. The old chief said that the snow was so deep and his village was so far down that it took a long time to climb out of it. After waiting still another day the expedition started for the Valley. When Tenaya was questioned as to the route and distance he said that the snow was so deep that the horses could not go through it. Old Tenaya was taken along as guide. When the party had gone about half-way to the Valley they met the Yosemites on their way to the camp on the south fork. There were only seventy-two of them and when the old chief was asked what had become of the rest of his band, he replied, "This is all of my people that are willing to go with me to the plains. All the rest have gone with their wives and children over the mountains to the Mono and Tuolumne tribes." Savage told Tenaya that he was not telling the truth, for Indians could not cross the mountains in the deep snow, and that he knew they must still be at his village or hiding somewhere near it. The tribe had been estimated to number over two hundred. Major Savage then said to him, "You may return to camp with your people and I will take one of your young men with me to your village to see your people who will not come. They will come if I find them." "You will not find any of my people there," said Tenaya; "I do not know where they are. My tribe is small. Many of the people of my tribe have come from other tribes and if they go to the plains and are seen they will be killed by the friends of those with whom they have quarreled. I was told that I was growing old and it was well that I should go, but that young and strong men can find plenty in the mountains: therefore, why should they go to the hot plains to be penned up like horses and cattle? My heart has been sore since that talk but I am now willing to go, for it is best for my people."

Pushing ahead, taking turns in breaking a way through the snow, they arrived in sight of the great Valley early in the afternoon and, guided by one of Tenaya's Indians, descended by the same route as that followed by the Mariposa trail, and the weary party went into camp on the river bank opposite El Capitan. After supper, seated around a big fire, the wonderful Valley became the topic of conversation and Dr. Bunell suggested giving it a name. Many were proposed, but after a vote had been taken the name Yosemite, proposed by Dr. Bunell, was adopted almost unanimously to perpetuate the name of the tribe who so long had made their home there. The Indian name of the Valley, however, is Ahwahnee. The Indians had names for all the different rocks and streams of the Valley, but very few of them are now in use by the whites, Pohono, the Bridal Veil, being the principal one. The expedition remained only one day and two nights in the Valley, hurrying out on the approach of a storm and reached the south-fork headquarters on the evening of the third day after starting out. Thus, in three days the round trip had been made to the Valley, most of it had been explored in a general way and some of its principal features had been named. But the Indians had fled up the Tenaya Cañon trail and none of them were seen, except an old woman unable to follow the fugitives.

A second expedition was made in the same year under command of Major Boling. When the Valley was entered no Indians were seen, but the many wigwams with smoldering fires showed that they had been hurriedly abandoned that very day. Later, five young Indians who had been left to watch the movements of the expedition were captured at the foot of the Three Brothers after a lively chase. Three of the five were sons of the old chief and the rock was named for them. All of these captives made good their escape within a few days, except the youngest son of Tenaya, who was shot by his guard while trying to escape. That same day the old chief was captured on the cliff on the east side of Indian Cañon by some of Boling's scouts. As Tenaya walked toward the camp his eye fell upon the dead body of his favorite son. Captain Boling through an interpreter, expressed his regret at the occurrence, but not a word did Tenaya utter in reply. Later, he made an attempt to escape but was caught as he was about to swim across the river. Tenaya expected to be shot for this attempt and when brought into the presence of Captain Boling he said in great emotion, "Kill me, Sir Captain, yes, kill me as you killed my son, as you would kill my people if they were to come to you. You would kill all my tribe if you had the power. Yes, Sir America, you can now tell your warriors to kill the old chief. You have made my life dark with sorrow. You killed the child of my heart. Why not kill the father? But wait a little and when I am dead I will call my people to come and they shall hear me in their sleep and come to avenge the death of their chief and his son. Yes, Sir America, my spirit will make trouble for you and your people, as you have made trouble to me and my people. With the wizards I will follow the white people and make them fear me. You may kill me, Sir Captain, but you shall not live in peace. I will follow in your footsteps. I will not leave my home, but be with the spirits among the rocks, the waterfalls, in the rivers and in the winds; wherever you go I will be with you. You will not see me but you will fear the spirit of the old chief and grow cold. The Great Spirit has spoken. I am done."

This expedition finally captured the remnants of the tribes at the head of Lake Tenaya and took them to the Fresno reservation, together with their chief, Tenaya. But after a short stay they were allowed to return to the Valley under restrictions. Tenaya promised faithfully to conform to everything required, joyfully left the hot and dry reservation, and with his family returned to his Yosemite home.

The following year a party of miners was attacked by the Indians in the Valley and two of them were killed. This led to another Yosemite expedition. A detachment of regular soldiers from Fort Miller under Lieutenant Moore, U.S.A., was at once dispatched to capture or punish the murderers. Lieutenant Moore entered the Valley in the night and surprised and captured a party of five Indians, but an alarm was given and Tenaya and his people fled from their huts and escaped to the Monos on the east side of the Range. On examination of the five prisoners in the morning it was discovered that each of them had some article of clothing that belonged to the murdered men. The bodies of the two miners were found and buried on the edge of the Bridal Veil meadow. When the captives were accused of the murder of the two white men they admitted that they had killed them to prevent white men from coming to their Valley, declaring that it was their home and that white men had no right to come there without their consent. Lieutenant Moore told them through his interpreter that they had sold their lands to the Government, that it belonged to the white men now, and that they had agreed to live on the reservation provided for them. To this they replied that Tenaya had never consented to the sale of their Valley and had never received pay for it. The other chief, they said, had no right to sell their territory. The lieutenant being fully satisfied that he had captured the real murderers, promptly pronounced judgment and had them placed in line and shot. Lieutenant Moore pursued the fugitives to Mono but was not successful in finding any of them. After being hospitably entertained and protected by the Mono and Paute tribes, they stole a number of stolen horses from their entertainers and made their way by a long, obscure route by the head of the north fork of the San Joaquin, reached their Yosemite home once more, but early one morning, after a feast of horse-flesh, a band of Monos surprised them in their huts, killing Tenaya and nearly all his tribe. Only a small remnant escaped down the river cañon. The Tenaya Cañon and Lake were named for the famous old chief.

Very few visits were made to the Valley before the summer of 1855, when Mr. J. M. Hutchings, having heard of its wonderful scenery, collected a party and made the first regular tourist's visit to the Yosemite and in his California magazine described it in articles illustrated by a good artist, who was taken into the Valley by him for that purpose. This first party was followed by another from Mariposa the same year, consisting of sixteen or eighteen persons. The next year the regular pleasure travel began and a trail on the Mariposa side of the Valley was opened by Mann Brothers. This trail was afterwards purchased by the citizens of the county and made free to the public. The first house built in the Yosemite Valley was erected in the autumn of 1856 and was kept as a hotel the next year by G. A. Hite and later by J. H. Neal and S. M. Cunningham. It was situated directly opposite the Yosemite Fall. A little over half a mile farther up the Valley a canvas house was put up in 1858 by G. A. Hite. Next year a frame house was built and kept as a hotel by Mr. Peck, afterward by Mr. Longhurst and since 1864 by Mr. Hutchings. All these hotels have vanished except the frame house built in 1859, which has been changed beyond recognition. A large hotel built on the brink of the river in front of the old one is now the only hotel in the Valley. A large hotel built by the State and located farther up the Valley was burned. To provide for the overflow of visitors there are three camps with board floors, wood frame, and covered with canvas, well furnished, some of them with electric light. A large first-class hotel is very much needed.

Travel of late years has been rapidly increasing, especially after the establishment, by Act of Congress in 1890, of the Yosemite National Park and the recession in 1905 of the original reservation to the Federal Government by the State. The greatest increase, of course, was caused by the construction of the Yosemite Valley railroad from Merced to the border of the Park, eight miles below the Valley.

It is eighty miles long, and the entire distance, except the first twenty-four miles from the town of Merced, is built through the precipitous Merced River Cañon. The roadbed was virtually blasted out of the solid rock for the entire distance in the cañon.

The Yosemite

Work was begun in September, 1905, and the first train entered El Portal, the terminus, April 15, 1907. Many miles of the road cost as much as $100,000 per mile. Its business has increased from 4000 tourists in the first year it was operated to 15,000 in 1910.

13

Lamon

THE good old pioneer, Lamon, was the first of all the early Yosemite settlers who cordially and unreservedly adopted the Valley as his home.

He was born in the Shenandoah Valley, Virginia, May 10, 1817, emigrated to Illinois with his father, John Lamon, at the age of nineteen; afterwards went to Texas and settled on the Brazos, where he raised melons and hunted alligators for a living. "Right interestin' business," he said; "especially the alligator part of it." From the Brazos he went to the Comanche Indian country between Gonzales and Austin, twenty miles from his nearest neighbor. During the first summer, the only bread he had was the breast meat of wild turkeys. When the formidable Comanche Indians were on the war-path he left his cabin after dark and slept in the woods. From Texas he crossed the plains to California and worked in the Calaveras and Mariposa gold-fields.

He first heard Yosemite spoken of as a very beautiful mountain valley and after making two excursions in the summers of 1857 and 1858 to see the wonderful place, he made up his mind to quit roving and make a permanent home in it. In April, 1859, he moved into it, located a garden opposite the Half Dome, set out a lot of apple, pear and peach trees, planted potatoes, etc., that he had packed in on a "contrary old mule," and worked for his board in building a hotel which was afterwards purchased by Mr. Hutchings. His neighbors thought he was very foolish in attempting to raise crops in so high and cold a valley, and warned him that he could raise nothing and sell nothing, and would surely starve.

For the first year or two lack of provisions compelled him to move out on the approach of winter, but in 1862 after he had succeeded in raising some fruit and vegetables he began to winter in the Valley.

The first winter he had no companions, not even a dog or cat, and one evening was greatly surprised to see two men coming up the Valley. They were very glad to see him, for they had come from Mariposa in search of him, a report having been spread that he had been killed by Indians. He assured his visitors that he felt safer in his Yosemite home, lying snug and squirrel-like in his 10 × 12 cabin, than in Mariposa. When the avalanches began to slip, he wondered where all the wild roaring and booming came from, the flying snow preventing them from being seen. But, upon the whole, he wondered most at the brightness, gentleness, and sunniness of the weather, and hopefully employed the calm days in clearing ground for an orchard and vegetable garden.

In the second winter he built a winter cabin under the Royal Arches, where he enjoyed more sunshine. But no matter how he praised the weather he could not induce any one to winter with him until 1864.

He liked to describe the great flood of 1867, the year before I reached California, when all the walls were striped with thundering waterfalls.

He was a fine, erect, whole-souled man, between six and seven feet high, with a broad, open face, bland and guileless as his pet oxen. No stranger to hunger and weariness, he knew well how to appreciate suffering of a like kind in others, and many there be, myself among the number, who can testify to his simple, unostentatious kindness that found expression in a thousand small deeds.

After gaining sufficient means to enjoy a long afternoon of life in comparative affluence and ease, he died in the autumn of 1876. He sleeps in a beautiful spot near Galen Clark and a monument hewn from a block of Yosemite granite marks his grave.

14

Galen Clark

GALEN CLARK was the best mountaineer I ever met, and one of the kindest and most amiable of all my mountain friends. I first met him at his Wawona ranch forty-three years ago on my first visit to Yosemite. I had entered the Valley with one companion by way of Coulterville, and returned by what was then known as the Mariposa trail. Both trails were buried in deep snow where the elevation was from 5000 to 7000 feet above sea level in the sugar pine and silver fir regions. We had no great difficulty, however, in finding our way by the trends of the main features of the topography. Botanizing by the way, we made slow, plodding progress, and were again about out of provisions when we reached Clark's hospitable cabin at Wawona. He kindly furnished us with flour and a little sugar and tea, and my companion, who complained of the benumbing poverty of a strictly vegetarian diet, gladly accepted Mr. Clark's offer of a piece of a bear that had just been killed. After a short talk about bears and the forests and the way to the Big Trees, we pushed on up through the Wawona firs and sugar pines, and camped in the now-famous Mariposa grove.

Later, after making my home in the Yosemite Valley, I became well acquainted with Mr. Clark, while he was guardian. He was elected again and again to this important office by different Boards of Commissioners on account of his efficiency and his real love of the Valley.

Although nearly all my mountaineering has been done with-

Galen Clark

out companions, I had the pleasure of having Galen Clark with me on three excursions. About thirty-five years ago I invited him to accompany me on a trip through the Big Tuolumne Cañon from Hetch Hetchy Valley. The cañon up to that time had not been explored, and knowing that the difference in the elevation of the river at the head of the cañon and in Hetch Hetchy was about 5000 feet, we expected to find some magnificent cataracts or falls; nor were we disappointed. When we were leaving Yosemite an ambitious young man begged leave to join us. I strongly advised him not to attempt such a long, hard trip, for it would undoubtedly prove very trying to an inexperienced climber. He assured us, however, that he was equal to anything, would gladly meet every difficulty as it came, and cause us no hindrance or trouble of any sort. So at last, after repeating our advice that he give up the trip, we consented to his joining us. We entered the cañon by way of Hetch Hetchy Valley, each carrying his own provisions, and making his own tea, porridge, bed, etc.

In the morning of the second day out from Hetch Hetchy we came to what is now known as "Muir Gorge," and Mr. Clark without hesitation prepared to force a way through it, wading and jumping from one submerged boulder to another through the torrent, bracing and steadying himself with a long pole. Though the river was then rather low, the savage, roaring, surging song it was singing was rather nerve-trying, especially to our inexperienced companion. With careful assistance, however, I managed to get him through, but this hard trial, naturally enough, proved too much and he informed us, pale and trembling, that he could go no farther. I gathered some wood at the upper throat of the gorge, made a fire for him and advised him to feel at home and make himself comfortable, hoped he would enjoy the grand scenery and the songs of the water-ouzels which haunted the gorge, and assured him that we would return some time in the night, though it might be late, as we wished to go on through the entire cañon if possible. We pushed our way through the dense chaparral and over the earthquake taluses with such speed that we reached the foot of the upper cataract while we had still an hour or so of daylight for the return trip. It was long after dark when we reached our adventurous, but nerve-shaken companion who, of course, was anxious and lonely, not being accustomed to solitude, however kindly and flowery and full of sweet bird-song and stream-song. Being tired we simply lay down in restful comfort on the river bank beside a good fire, instead of trying to go down the gorge in the dark or climb over its high shoulder to our blankets and provisions, which we had left in the morning in a tree at the foot of the gorge. I remember Mr. Clark remarking that if he had his choice that night between provisions and blankets he would choose his blankets.

The next morning in about an hour we had crossed over the ridge through which the gorge is cut, reached our provisions, made tea, and had a good breakfast. As soon as we had returned to Yosemite I obtained fresh provisions, pushed off alone up to the head of Yosemite Creek basin, entered the cañon by a side cañon, and completed the exploration up to the Tuolumne Meadows.

It was on this first trip from Hetch Hetchy to the upper cataracts that I had convincing proofs of Mr. Clark's daring and skill as a mountaineer, particularly in fording torrents, and in forcing his way through thick chaparral. I found it somewhat difficult to keep up with him in dense, tangled brush, though in jumping on boulder taluses and slippery cobble-beds I had no difficulty in leaving him behind.

Galen Clark

After I had discovered the glaciers on Mount Lyell and Mount McClure, Mr. Clark kindly made a second excursion with me to assist in establishing a line of stakes across the McClure glacier to measure its rate of flow. On this trip we also climbed Mount Lyell together, when the snow which covered the glacier was melted into upleaning, icy blades which were extremely difficult to cross, not being strong enough to support our weight, nor wide enough apart to enable us to stride across each blade as it was met. Here again I, being lighter, had no difficulty in keeping ahead of him. While resting after wearisome staggering and falling he stared at the mar- velous ranks of leaning blades, and said, "I think I have traveled all sorts of trails and cañons, through all kinds of brush and snow, but this gets me."

Mr. Clark at my urgent request joined my small party on a trip to the Kings River yosemite by way of the high mountains, most of the way without a trail. He joined us at the Mariposa Big Tree grove and intended to go all the way, but finding that, on account of the difficulties encountered, the time required was much greater than he expected, he turned back near the head of the north fork of the Kings River.

In cooking his mess of oatmeal porridge and making tea, his pot was always the first to boil, and I used to wonder why, with all his skill in scrambling through brush in the easiest way, and pre- paring his meals, he was so utterly careless about his beds. He would lie down anywhere on any ground, rough or smooth, with- out taking pains even to remove cobbles or sharp-angled rocks pro- truding through the grass or gravel, saying that his own bones were as hard as any stones and could do him no harm.

His kindness to all Yosemite visitors and mountaineers was

marvelously constant and uniform. He was not a good business man, and in building an extensive hotel and barns at Wawona, before the travel to Yosemite had been greatly developed, he borrowed money, mortgaged his property and lost it all.

Though not the first to see the Mariposa Big Tree grove, he was the first to explore it, after he had heard from a prospector, who had passed through the grove and who gave him the indefinite information, that there were some wonderful big trees up there on the top of the Wawona hill and that he believed they must be of the same kind that had become so famous and well-known in the Calaveras grove farther north. On this information, Galen Clark told me, he went up and thoroughly explored the grove, counting the trees and measuring the largest, and becoming familiar with it. He stated also that he had explored the forest to the southward and had discovered the much larger Fresno grove of about two square miles, six or seven miles distant from the Mariposa grove. Unfortunately most of the Fresno grove has been cut and flumed down to the railroad near Madera.

Mr. Clark was truly and literally a gentle-man. I never heard him utter a hasty, angry, fault-finding word. His voice was uniformly pitched at a rather low tone, perfectly even, although glances of his eyes and slight intonations of his voice often indicated that something funny or mildly sarcastic was coming, but upon the whole he was serious and industrious, and, however deep and fun-provoking a story might be, he never indulged in boisterous laughter.

He was very fond of scenery and once told me after I became acquainted with him that he liked "nothing in the world better than climbing to the top of a high ridge or mountain and looking off."

Galen Clark

He preferred the mountain ridges and domes in the Yosemite regions on account of the wealth and beauty of the forests. Oftentimes he would take his rifle, a few pounds of bacon, a few pounds of flour, and a single blanket and go off hunting, for no other reason than to explore and get acquainted with the most beautiful points of view within a journey of a week or two from his Wawona home. On these trips he was always alone and could indulge in tranquil enjoyment of Nature to his heart's content. He said that on those trips, when he was a sufficient distance from home in a neighborhood where he wished to linger, he always shot a deer, sometimes a grouse, and occasionally a bear. After diminishing the weight of a deer or bear by eating part of it, he carried as much as possible of the best of the meat to Wawona, and from his hospitable well-supplied cabin no weary wanderer ever went away hungry or unrested.

The value of the mountain air in prolonging life is well exemplified in Mr. Clark's case. While working in the mines he contracted a severe cold that settled on his lungs and finally caused severe inflammation and bleeding, and none of his friends thought he would ever recover. The physicians told him he had but a short time to live. It was then that he repaired to the beautiful sugar pine woods at Wawona and took up a claim, including the fine meadows there, and building his cabin, began his life of wandering and exploring in the glorious mountains about him, usually going bareheaded. In a remarkably short time his lungs were healed.

He was one of the most sincere tree-lovers I ever knew. About twenty years before his death he made choice of a plot in the Yosemite cemetery on the north side of the Valley, not far from the Yosemite Fall, and selecting a dozen or so of seedling sequoias in

[185]

the Mariposa grove he brought them to the Valley and planted them around the spot he had chosen for his last rest. The ground there is gravelly and dry; by careful watering he finally nursed most of the seedlings into good, thrifty trees, and doubtless they will long shade the grave of their blessed lover and friend.

15

Hetch Hetchy Valley

YOSEMITE is so wonderful that we are apt to regard it as an exceptional creation, the only valley of its kind in the world; but Nature is not so poor as to have only one of anything. Several other yosemites have been discovered in the Sierra that occupy the same relative positions on the Range and were formed by the same forces in the same kind of granite. One of these, the Hetch Hetchy Valley, is in the Yosemite National Park about twenty miles from Yosemite and is easily accessible to all sorts of travelers by a road and trail that leaves the Big Oak Flat road at Bronson Meadows a few miles below Crane Flat, and to mountaineers by way of Yosemite Creek basin and the head of the middle fork of the Tuolumne.

It is said to have been discovered by Joseph Screech, a hunter, in 1850, a year before the discovery of the great Yosemite. After my first visit to it in the autumn of 1871, I have always called it the "Tuolumne Yosemite," for it is a wonderfully exact counterpart of the Merced Yosemite, not only in its sublime rocks and waterfalls but in the gardens, groves and meadows of its flowery park-like floor. The floor of Yosemite is about 4000 feet above the sea; the Hetch Hetchy floor about 3700 feet. And as the Merced River flows through Yosemite, so does the Tuolumne through Hetch Hetchy. The walls of both are of gray granite, rise abruptly from the floor, are sculptured in the same style and in both every rock is a glacier monument.

Standing boldly out from the south wall is a strikingly picturesque rock called by the Indians, Kolana, the outermost of a group 2300 feet high, corresponding with the Cathedral Rocks of Yosemite both in relative position and form. On the opposite side of the Valley, facing Kolana, there is a counterpart of the El Capitan that rises sheer and plain to a height of 1800 feet, and over its massive brow flows a stream which makes the most graceful fall I have ever seen. From the edge of the cliff to the top of an earthquake talus it is perfectly free in the air for a thousand feet before it is broken into cascades among talus boulders. It is in all its glory in June, when the snow is melting fast, but fades and vanishes toward the end of summer. The only fall I know with which it may fairly be compared is the Yosemite Bridal Veil; but it excels even that favorite fall both in height and airy-fairy beauty and behavior. Lowlanders are apt to suppose that mountain streams in their wild career over cliffs lose control of themselves and tumble in a noisy chaos of mist and spray. On the contrary, on no part of their travels are they more harmonious and self-controlled. Imagine yourself in Hetch Hetchy on a sunny day in June, standing waist-deep in grass and flowers (as I have often stood), while the great pines sway dreamily with scarcely perceptible motion. Looking northward across the Valley you see a plain, gray granite cliff rising abruptly out of the gardens and groves to a height of 1800 feet, and in front of it Tueeulala's silvery scarf burning with irised sun-fire. In the first white outburst at the head there is abundance of visible energy, but it is speedily hushed and concealed in divine repose, and its tranquil progress to the base of the cliff is like that of a downy feather in a still room. Now observe the fineness and marvelous distinctness of the various sun-illumined fabrics into which the water is woven; they sift and float from form to form down the face of that grand gray rock in so leisurely and unconfused a manner that you can examine their texture, and patterns and tones of color as you would a piece of embroidery held in the hand. Toward the top of the fall you see groups of booming, comet-like masses, their solid, white heads separate, their tails like combed silk interlacing among delicate gray and purple shadows, ever forming and dissolving, worn out by friction in their rush through the air. Most of these vanish a few hundred feet below the summit, changing to varied forms of cloud-like drapery. Near the bottom the width of the fall has increased from about twenty-five feet to a hundred feet. Here it is composed of yet finer tissues, and is still without a trace of disorder—air, water and sunlight woven into stuff that spirits might wear.

So fine a fall might well seem sufficient to glorify any valley; but here, as in Yosemite, Nature seems in nowise moderate, for a short distance to the eastward of Tueeulala booms and thunders the great Hetch Hetchy Fall, Wapama, so near that you have both of them in full view from the same standpoint. It is the counterpart of the Yosemite Fall, but has a much greater volume of water, is about 1700 feet in height, and appears to be nearly vertical, though considerably inclined, and is dashed into huge outbounding bosses of foam on projecting shelves and knobs. No two falls could be more unlike—Tueeulala out in the open sunshine descending like thistledown; Wapama in a jagged, shadowy gorge roaring and thundering, pounding its way like an earthquake avalanche.

Besides this glorious pair there is a broad, massive fall on the main river a short distance above the head of the Valley. Its position is something like that of the Vernal in Yosemite, and its roar as it plunges into a surging trout-pool may be heard a long way, though it is only about twenty feet high. On Rancheria Creek, a large stream, corresponding in position with the Yosemite Tenaya Creek, there is a chain of cascades joined here and there with swift flashing plumes like the one between the Vernal and Nevada Falls, making magnificent shows as they go their glacier-sculptured way, sliding, leaping, hurrahing, covered with crisp clashing spray made glorious with sifting sunshine. And besides all these a few small streams come over the walls at wide intervals, leaping from ledge to ledge with birdlike song and watering many a hidden cliff-garden and fernery, but they are too unshowy to be noticed in so grand a place.

The correspondence between the Hetch Hetchy walls in their trends, sculpture, physical structure, and general arrangement of the main rock-masses and those of the Yosemite Valley has excited the wondering admiration of every observer. We have seen that the El Capitan and Cathedral rocks occupy the same relative positions in both valleys; so also do their Yosemite points and North Domes. Again, that part of the Yosemite north wall immediately to the east of the Yosemite Fall has two horizontal benches, about 500 and 1500 feet above the floor, timbered with golden-cup oak. Two benches similarly situated and timbered occur on the same relative portion of the Hetch Hetchy north wall, to the east of Wapama Fall, and on no other. The Yosemite is bounded at the head by the great Half Dome. Hetch Hetchy is bounded in the same way, though its head rock is incomparably less wonderful and sublime in form.

The floor of the Valley is about three and a half miles long, and from a fourth to half a mile wide. The lower portion is mostly a level meadow about a mile long, with the trees restricted to the sides and the river banks, and partially separated from the main, upper, forested portion by a low bar of glacier-polished granite across which the river breaks in rapids.

The principal trees are the yellow and sugar pines, digger pine, incense cedar, Douglas spruce, silver fir, the California and golden-cup oaks, balsam cottonwood, Nuttall's flowering dogwood, alder, maple, laurel, tumion, etc. The most abundant and influential are the great yellow or silver pines like those of Yosemite, the tallest over two hundred feet in height, and the oaks assembled in magnificent groves with massive rugged trunks four to six feet in diameter, and broad, shady, wide-spreading heads. The shrubs forming conspicuous flowery clumps and tangles are manzanita, azalea, spiræa, brier-rose, several species of ceanothus, calycanthus, philadelphus, wild cherry, etc.; with abundance of showy and fragrant herbaceous plants growing about them or out in the open in beds by themselves—lilies, Mariposa tulips, brodiaeas, orchids, iris, spraguea, draperia, collomia, collinsia, castilleja, nemophila, larkspur, columbine, goldenrods, sunflowers, mints of many species, honeysuckle, etc. Many fine ferns dwell here also, especially the beautiful and interesting rock-ferns—pellaea, and cheilanthes of several species—fringing and rosetting dry rock-piles and ledges; woodwardia and asplenium on damp spots with fronds six or seven feet high; the delicate maidenhair in mossy nooks by the falls, and the sturdy, broad-shouldered pteris covering nearly all the dry ground beneath the oaks and pines.

It appears, therefore, that Hetch Hetchy Valley, far from being a plain, common, rock-bound meadow, as many who have not seen it seem to suppose, is a grand landscape garden, one of Nature's rarest and most precious mountain temples. As in Yosemite, the sublime rocks of its walls seem to glow with life, whether leaning back in repose or standing erect in thoughtful attitudes, giving welcome to storms and calms alike, their brows in the sky, their feet set in the groves and gay flowery meadows, while birds, bees, and butterflies help the river and waterfalls to stir all the air into music—things frail and fleeting and types of permanence meeting here and blending, just as they do in Yosemite, to draw her lovers into close and confiding communion with her.

Sad to say, this most precious and sublime feature of the Yosemite National Park, one of the greatest of all our natural resources for the uplifting joy and peace and health of the people, is in danger of being dammed and made into a reservoir to help supply San Francisco with water and light, thus flooding it from wall to wall and burying its gardens and groves one or two hundred feet deep. This grossly destructive commercial scheme has long been planned and urged (though water as pure and abundant can be got from outside of the people's park, in a dozen different places), because of the comparative cheapness of the dam and of the territory which it is sought to divert from the great uses to which it was dedicated in the Act of 1890 establishing the Yosemite National Park.

The making of gardens and parks goes on with civilization all over the world, and they increase both in size and number as their value is recognized. Everybody needs beauty as well as bread, places to play in and pray in, where Nature may heal and cheer and give strength to body and soul alike. This natural beauty-hunger is made manifest in the little window-sill gardens of the poor, though perhaps only a geranium slip in a broken cup, as well as in the carefully tended rose and lily gardens of the rich, the thousands of spacious city parks and botanical gardens, and in our

Hetch Hetchy Valley

magnificent National parks—the Yellowstone, Yosemite, Sequoia, etc.—Nature's sublime wonderlands, the admiration and joy of the world. Nevertheless, like anything else worth while, from the very beginning, however well guarded, they have always been subject to attack by despoiling gainseekers and mischief-makers of every degree from Satan to Senators, eagerly trying to make everything immediately and selfishly commercial, with schemes disguised in smug-smiling philanthropy, industriously, shampiously crying, "Conservation, conservation, panutilization," that man and beast may be fed and the dear Nation made great. Thus long ago a few enterprising merchants utilized the Jerusalem temple as a place of business instead of a place of prayer, changing money, buying and selling cattle and sheep and doves; and earlier still, the first forest reservation, including only one tree, was likewise despoiled. Ever since the establishment of the Yosemite National Park, strife has been going on around its borders and I suppose this will go on as part of the universal battle between right and wrong, however much its boundaries may be shorn, or its wild beauty destroyed.

The first application to the Government by the San Francisco Supervisors for the commercial use of Lake Eleanor and the Hetch Hetchy Valley was made in 1903, and on December 22nd of that year it was denied by the Secretary of the Interior, Mr. Hitchcock, who truthfully said:

Presumably the Yosemite National Park was created such by law because of the natural objects of varying degrees of scenic importance located within its boundaries, inclusive alike of its beautiful small lakes, like

The Yosemite

Eleanor, and its majestic wonders, like Hetch Hetchy and Yosemite Valley. It is the aggregation of such natural scenic features that makes the Yosemite Park a wonderland which the Congress of the United States sought by law to reserve for all coming time as nearly as practicable in the condition fashioned by the hand of the Creator—a worthy object of national pride and a source of healthful pleasure and rest for the thousands of people who may annually sojourn there during the heated months.

In 1907 when Mr. Garfield became Secretary of the Interior the application was renewed and granted; but under his successor, Mr. Fisher, the matter has been referred to a Commission, which as this volume goes to press still has it under consideration.

The most delightful and wonderful camp grounds in the Park are its three great valleys—Yosemite, Hetch Hetchy, and Upper Tuolumne; and they are also the most important places with reference to their positions relative to the other great features—the Merced and Tuolumne Cañons, and the High Sierra peaks and glaciers, etc., at the head of the rivers. The main part of the Tuolumne Valley is a spacious flowery lawn four or five miles long, surrounded by magnificent snowy mountains, slightly separated from other beautiful meadows, which together make a series about twelve miles in length, the highest reaching to the feet of Mount Dana, Mount Gibbs, Mount Lyell and Mount McClure. It is about 8500 feet above the sea, and forms the grand central High Sierra camp ground from which excursions are made to the noble mountains, domes, glaciers, etc.; across the Range to the Mono Lake and volcanoes and down the Tuolumne Cañon to Hetch Het-

Hetch Hetchy Valley

chy. Should Hetch Hetchy be submerged for a reservoir, as proposed, not only would it be utterly destroyed, but the sublime cañon way to the heart of the High Sierra would be hopelessly blocked and the great camping ground, as the watershed of a city drinking system, virtually would be closed to the public. So far as I have learned, few of all the thousands who have seen the park and seek rest and peace in it are in favor of this outrageous scheme.

One of my later visits to the Valley was made in the autumn of 1907 with the late William Keith, the artist. The leaf-colors were then ripe, and the great godlike rocks in repose seemed to glow with life. The artist, under their spell, wandered day after day along the river and through the groves and gardens, studying the wonderful scenery; and, after making about forty sketches, declared with enthusiasm that although its walls were less sublime in height, in picturesque beauty and charm Hetch Hetchy surpassed even Yosemite.

That any one would try to destroy such a place seems incredible; but sad experience shows that there are people good enough and bad enough for anything. The proponents of the dam scheme bring forward a lot of bad arguments to prove that the only righteous thing to do with the people's parks is to destroy them bit by bit as they are able. Their arguments are curiously like those of the devil, devised for the destruction of the first garden—so much of the very best Eden fruit going to waste; so much of the best Tuolumne water and Tuolumne scenery going to waste. Few of their statements are even partly true, and all are misleading.

Thus, Hetch Hetchy, they say, is a "low-lying meadow." On the contrary, it is a high-lying natural landscape garden, as the photographic illustrations show.

The Yosemite

"It is a common minor feature, like thousands of others." On the contrary it is a very uncommon feature; after Yosemite, the rarest and in many ways the most important in the National Park.

"Damming and submerging it 175 feet deep would enhance its beauty by forming a crystal-clear lake." Landscape gardens, places of recreation and worship, are never made beautiful by destroying and burying them. The beautiful sham lake, forsooth, would be only an eyesore, a dismal blot on the landscape, like many others to be seen in the Sierra. For, instead of keeping it at the same level all the year, allowing Nature centuries of time to make new shores, it would, of course, be full only a month or two in the spring, when the snow is melting fast; then it would be gradually drained, exposing the slimy sides of the basin and shallower parts of the bottom, with the gathered drift and waste, death and decay of the upper basins, caught here instead of being swept on to decent natural burial along the banks of the river or in the sea. Thus the Hetch Hetchy dam-lake would be only a rough imitation of a natural lake for a few of the spring months, an open sepulcher for the others.

"Hetch Hetchy water is the purest of all to be found in the Sierra, unpolluted, and forever unpollutable." On the contrary, excepting that of the Merced below Yosemite, it is less pure than that of most of the other Sierra streams, because of the sewerage of camp grounds draining into it, especially of the Big Tuolumne Meadows camp ground, occupied by hundreds of tourists and mountaineers, with their animals, for months every summer, soon to be followed by thousands from all the world.

These temple destroyers, devotees of ravaging commercialism, seem to have a perfect contempt for Nature, and, instead of

Hetch Hetchy Valley

lifting their eyes to the God of the mountains, lift them to the Almighty Dollar.

Dam Hetch Hetchy! As well dam for water-tanks the people's cathedrals and churches, for no holier temple has ever been consecrated by the heart of man.

APPENDIX A

Legislation About the Yosemite

In the year 1864, Congress passed the following act:—

ACT OF JUNE 30, 1864 (13 STAT., 325).

AN ACT Authorizing a grant to the State of California of the "Yo-Semite Valley," and of the land embracing the "Mariposa Big Tree Grove."

"Be it enacted by the Senate and House of Representatives of the United States of America, in Congress assembled, That there shall be, and is hereby, granted to the State of California, the 'Cleft' or 'Gorge' in the Granite Peak of the Sierra Nevada Mountains, situated in the county of Mariposa, in the State aforesaid, and the headwaters of the Merced River, and known as the Yosemite Valley, with its branches and spurs, in estimated length fifteen miles, and in average width one mile back from the main edge of the precipice, on each side of the Valley, with the stipulation, nevertheless, that the said State shall accept this grant upon the express conditions that the premises shall be held for public use, resort, and recreation; shall be inalienable for all time; but leases not exceeding ten years may be granted for portions of said premises. All incomes derived from leases of privileges to be expended in the preservation and improvement of the property, or the roads leading thereto; the boundaries to be established at the cost of said State by the United States Surveyor-General of California, whose official plat, when affirmed by the Commissioner of the General Land Office, shall constitute the evidence of the locus, extent, and limits of the said Cleft or Gorge; the premises to be managed by the Governor of the State, with eight other Commissioners,

Appendix A

to be appointed by the Executive of California, and who shall receive no compensation for their services.

"SEC. 2. *And be it further enacted*, That there shall likewise be, and there is hereby, granted to the said State of California, the tracts embracing what is known as the 'Mariposa Big Tree Grove,' not to exceed the area of four sections, and to be taken in legal subdivisions of one-quarter section each, with the like stipulations as expressed in the first section of this Act as to the State's acceptance, with like conditions as in the first section of this Act as to inalienability, yet with the same lease privileges; the income to be expended in the preservation, improvement, and protection of the property, the premises to be managed by Commissioners, as stipulated in the first section of this Act, and to be taken in legal subdivisions as aforesaid; and the official plat of the United States Surveyor-General, when affirmed by the Commissioner of the General Land Office, to be the evidence of the locus of the said Mariposa Big Tree Grove."

This important act was approved by the President, June 30, 1864, and shortly after the Governor of California, F. F. Low, issued a proclamation taking possession of the Yosemite Valley and Mariposa grove of Big Trees, in the name and on behalf of the State, appointing commissioners to manage them, and warning all persons against trespassing or settling there without authority, and especially forbidding the cutting of timber and other injurious acts.

The first Board of Commissioners were F. Law Olmsted, J. D. Whitney, William Ashburner, I. W. Raymond, E. S. Holden, Alexander Deering, George W. Coulter, and Galen Clark.

Appendix A

ACT OF OCTOBER 1, 1890 (26 STAT., 650).[1]

AN ACT To set apart certain tracts of land in the State of California as forest reservations.

"Be it enacted by the Senate and House of Representatives of the United States of America in Congress assembled, That the tracts of land in the State of California known as described as follows: Commencing at the northwest corner of township two north, range nineteen east Mount Diablo meridian, thence eastwardly on the line between townships two and three north, ranges twenty-four and twenty-five east; thence southwardly on the line between ranges twenty-four and twenty-five east to the Mount Diablo base line; thence eastwardly on said base line to the corner to township one south, ranges twenty-five and twenty-six east; thence southwardly on the line between ranges twenty-five and twenty-six east to the southeast corner of township two south, range twenty-five east; thence eastwardly on the line between townships two and three south, range twenty-six east to the corner to townships two and three south, ranges twenty-six and twenty-seven east; thence southwardly on the line between ranges twenty-six and twenty-seven east to the first standard parallel south; thence westwardly on the first standard parallel south to the southwest corner of township four south, range nineteen east; thence northwardly on the line between ranges eighteen and nineteen east to the northwest corner of township two south, range nineteen east; thence westwardly on the line between townships one and two south to the southwest corner of township one south, range nineteen east; thence northwardly on the line between ranges eighteen and nineteen east to the northwest corner of township two north, range nineteen east, the place of beginning, are hereby reserved and withdrawn from settlement, occupancy, or sale un-

[1] Sections 1 and 2 of this act pertain to the Yosemite National Park, while section 3 sets apart General Grant National Park, and also a portion of Sequoia National Park.

Appendix A

der the laws of the United States, and set apart as reserved forest lands; and all persons who shall locate or settle upon, or occupy the same or any part thereof, except as hereinafter provided, shall be considered trespassers and removed therefrom: *Provided, however,* That nothing in this act shall be construed as in anywise affecting the grant of lands made to the State of California by virtue of the act entitled, 'An act authorizing a grant to the State of California of the Yosemite Valley, and of the land embracing the Mariposa Big-Tree Grove, appeared June thirtieth, eighteen hundred and sixty-four; or as affecting any bona-fide entry of land made within the limits above described under any law of the United States prior to the approval of this act.

"SEC. 2. That said reservation shall be under the exclusive control of the Secretary of the Interior, whose duty it shall be, as soon as practicable, to make and publish such rules and regulations as he may deem necessary or proper for the care and management of the same. Such regulations shall provide for the preservation from injury of all timber, mineral deposits, natural curiosities, or wonders within said reservation, and their retention in their natural condition. The Secretary may, in his discretion, grant leases for building purposes for terms not exceeding ten years of small parcels of ground not exceeding five acres; at such places in said reservation as shall require the erection of buildings for the accommodation of visitors; all of the proceeds of said leases and other revenues that may be derived from any source connected with said reservation to be expended under his direction in the management of the same and the construction of roads and paths therein. He shall provide against the wanton destruction of the fish, and game found within said reservation, and against their capture or destruction, for the purposes of merchandise or profit. He shall also cause all persons trespassing upon the same after the passage of this act to be removed therefrom, and, generally, shall be authorized to take all such measures as shall be necessary or proper to fully carry out the objects and purposes of this act.

Appendix A

"SEC. 3. There shall also be and is hereby reserved and withdrawn from settlement, occupancy, or sale under the laws of the United States, and shall be set apart as reserved forest lands, as hereinbefore provided, and subject to all the limitations and provisions herein contained, the following additional lands, to wit: Township seventeen south, range thirty east of the Mount Diablo meridian, excepting sections thirty-one, thirty-two, thirty-three, and thirty-four of said township, included in a previous bill. And there is also reserved and withdrawn from settlement, occupancy, or sale under the laws of the United States, and set apart as forest lands, subject to like limitations, conditions, and provisions, all of townships fifteen and sixteen south, of ranges twenty-nine and thirty east of the Mount Diablo meridian. And there is also hereby reserved and withdrawn from settlement, occupancy, or sale under the laws of the United States, and set apart as reserved forest lands under like limitations, restrictions, and provisions, sections five and six in township fourteen south, range twenty-eight east of Mount Diablo meridian, and also sections thirty-one and thirty-two of township thirteen south, range twenty-eight east of the same meridian. Nothing in this act shall authorize rules or contracts touching the protection and improvement of said reservations, beyond the sums that may be received by the Secretary of the Interior under the foregoing provisions, or authorize any charge against the Treasury of the United States.

ACT OF THE LEGISLATURE OF THE STATE OF CALIFORNIA, APPROVED MARCH 3, 1905

"SEC. 1. The State of California does hereby recede and regrant unto the United States of America the 'cleft' or 'gorge' in the granite peak of the Sierra Nevada Mountains, situated in the county of Mariposa, State of California, and the headwaters of the Merced River, and known as the Yosemite Valley, with its branches and spurs, granted unto the State

Appendix A

of California in trust for public use, resort, and recreation by the act of Congress entitled, 'An act authorizing a grant to the State of California of the Yosemite Valley and of the land embracing the Mariposa Big Tree Grove,' approved June thirtieth, eighteen hundred and sixty-four; and the State of California does hereby relinquish unto the United States of America and resign the trusts created and granted by the said act of Congress.

"SEC. 2. The State of California does hereby recede and regrant unto the United States of America the tracts embracing what is known as the 'Mariposa Big Tree Grove,' planted unto the State of California in trust for public use, resort, and recreation by the act of Congress referred to in section one of this act, and the State of California does hereby relinquish unto the United States of America and resign the trusts created and granted by the said act of Congress.

"SEC. 3. This act shall take effect from and after acceptance by the United States of America of the recessions and regrants herein made, thereby forever releasing the State of California from further cost of maintaining the said premises, the same to be held for all time by the United States of America for public use, resort, and recreation and imposing on the United States of America the cost of maintaining the same as a national park: *Provided, however,* That the recession and regrant hereby made shall not affect vested rights and interests of third persons."

Table of Distances

From the Guardian's office, in the village, the distances to various points are in miles as follows:

	Miles.
Bridal Veil Fall	4.04
Cascade Falls	7.67
Cloud's Rest, Summit	11.81
Columbia Rock, on Eagle Peak Trail	1.98
Dana, Mt., Summit	40.34
Eagle Peak	6.59
El Capitan Bridge	3.63
Glacier Point, direct trail	4.45
Glacier Point, by Nevada Falls	16.98
Lyell, Mt., Summit	38.20
Merced Bridge	2.03
Mirror Lake, by Hunt's avenue	2.91
Nevada Fall (Hotel)	4.63
Nevada Fall, Bridge above	5.45
Pohono Bridge	5.29
Register Rock	3.24
Ribbon Fall	3.99
Rocky Point (base of Three Brothers)	1.45
Tenayah Creek Bridge	2.26
Tenayah Lake	16.00
Yosemite Falls, foot	0.90
Yosemite Falls, foot Upper Fall	2.67

Appendix B

Yosemite Falls, top   4.33
Soda Springs (Eagle Peak Trail)   24.50
Sentinel Dome   5.57
Union Point, on Glacier Point Trail   3.13
Vernal Fall   3.50

APPENDIX C

Maximum Rates for Transportation

The following rates for transportation in and about the Valley have been established by the Board of Commissioners:

From	Route to	Amount.
Valley	Glacier Point and Sentinel Dome, and return, direct, same day	$3.00
Valley	Glacier Point, Sentinel Dome, and Fissures, and return, direct, same day	3.75
Valley	Glacier Point, Sentinel Dome, and Fissures, passing night at Glacier Point	3.00
Valley	Glacier Point, Sentinel Dome, Nevada Fall, and Casa Nevada, passing night at Casa Nevada	3.00
Valley	Glacier Point, Sentinel Dome, Nevada Fall, Vernal Fall, and thence to Valley same day	4.00
Glacier Point	Valley direct	2.00
Glacier Point	Sentinel Dome, Nevada Fall, and Casa Nevada, passing night at Casa Nevada	2.00
Glacier Point	Sentinel Dome, Nevada Fall, Vernal Fall, and thence to Valley same day	3.00
Valley	Summits, Vernal and Nevada Falls, direct, and return to Valley same day	3.00
Valley	Glacier Point by Casa Nevada, passing night at Glacier Point	3.00
Valley	Summits, Vernal and Nevada Falls, Sentinel Dome, Glacier Point, and thence to Valley same day	4.00
Valley	Cloud's Rest and return to Casa Nevada	3.00

Appendix C

Valley	Cloud's Rest and return to Valley same day	5.00
Casa Nevada	Cloud's Rest and return to Casa Nevada or Valley same day	3.00
Casa Nevada	Valley direct	2.00
Casa Nevada	Nevada Fall, Sentinel Dome, and Glacier Point, passing night at Glacier Point	2.00
Valley	Nevada Fall, Sentinel Dome, Glacier Point, and Valley same day	3.00
	Upper Yosemite Fall, Eagle Peak, and return	3.00
	Charge for guide (including horse), when furnished	3.00
	Saddle-horses, on level of Valley, per day	2.50

1. The above charges do not include feed for horses when passing night at Casa Nevada or Glacier Point.

2. Where Valley is specified as starting-point, the above rates prevail from any hotel in Valley, or from the foot of any trail.

3. Any shortening of above trips, without proportionate reduction of rates, shall be at the option of those hiring horses.

4. Trips other than those above specified shall be subject to special arrangement between letter and hirer.

CARRIAGES

From	Route to	Amount.
Hotels	Mirror Lake and return, direct	$1.00
Hotels	Mirror Lake and return by Tissiack Avenue	1.25
Hotels	Mirror Lake and return to foot of Trail, to Vernal and Nevada Falls	1.00
Hotels	Bridal Veil Falls and return, direct	1.00
Hotels	Pohono Bridge, down either side of Valley, and return on opposite side, stopping at Yosemite and Bridal Veil Falls	1.50
Hotels	Cascade Falls, down either side of Valley, and return on opposite side, stopping at Yosemite and Bridal Veil Falls	2.25
Hotels	Artist Point and return, direct, stopping at Bridal Veil Fall	2.00

Appendix C

Hotels	New Inspiration Point and return, direct, stopping at Bridal Veil Falls	2.00
	Grand Round Drive, including Yosemite and Bridal Veil Falls, excluding Lake and Cascades	2.50
	Grand Round Drive, including Yosemite and Bridal Veil Falls, Lake, and Cascades	3.50

1. When the value of the seats hired in any vehicle shall exceed $15 for a two-horse team, or $25 for a four-horse team, *for any trip* in the above schedule, the persons hiring the seats shall have the privilege of paying no more than the aggregate sums of $15 and $25 *per trip* for a two-horse and four-horse team, respectively.

2. If saddle-horses should be substituted for any of the above carriage trips, carriage rates will apply to each horse. In no case shall the *per diem* charge of $2.50 for each saddle-horse, on level of Valley, be exceeded.

Any excess of the above rates, as well as *any* extortion, incivility, misrepresentation, or the riding of unsafe animals, should be promptly reported at the Guardian's office.

Index

Index

Index

Index

Pinus albicaulis (white-bark pine), 91–92, 126, 159
Pinus attenuata, 71–72
Pinus contorta, 83–85, 126
Pinus Lambertiana (sugar pine), 5, 6, 65, 69, 72–75, 78, 167
Pinus monophylla (nut pine), 92–93
Pinus monticola (mountain pine), 85–86
Pinus ponderosa (yellow pine), 65, 75–77
Pinus Sabiniana (nut pine), 69, 70–71
Pitt River basin, 76
Plants, 57, 191
Pohono basin, lakes in, 12
Pohono Canon, 135
Pohono. *See* Bridal Veil Fall
Poplar, 68
Populus trichocarpa (poplar), 68
Primula suffrutescens (wild primrose), 110
Pseudotsuga Douglasii (Douglas spruce), 5, 66, 69, 74, 78–79, 167, 191

Quercus agrifolia (California live-oak), 66
Quercus chrysolepis (mountain live-oak), 66–67, 190, 191

Railroad, 167, 175–76
Rancheria Creek, 189–90
Red Mountain, 142; glaciers and, 151–53
Ribbon Creek basin, 147, 148
Ribbon Fall, 7–8, 147, 148
River Canon, 145
Robins, 117, 118–19, 121
Roses: brier, 112, 191; prim-, 110; wild, 75, 112, 113–14
Royal Arches, 9, 126, 145–46; cabin under, 178
Royal Arch Fall, 26, 41, 42
Rubus nutkanus, 112, 114

San Joaquin River, 106, 146, 161–62; basin, 143–44
Santa Clara Valley, 2
Sarcodes sanguinea (snow plant), 75, 111
Savage, Major, 168–71
Screech, Joseph, 187

Sentinel Canon, 135
Sentinel Cascades, 26, 40, 41, 42
Sentinel Rock (Dome), 8, 58, 135, 145, 146, 147, 148, 165; yellow pines near, 65
Sequoia gigantea (giant sequoia). *See* Sequoias
Sequoia National Park, 95, 108
Sequoias, 5–6, 69, 74; described, 96–100; distribution of, 100, 101–103, 105–107; glacial action and, 105–107; groves of, *see* specific names of groves; life of, 100–101, 107–109; location of, 94–96, 108–109; streams and, 104–105
Shrubs, 191
Sierra Cathedral, 10–11
Sierra Mountains, 2–3
Silver pine. *See* Pine, yellow
Snow, 157–58; banners, 52–64; storms, 32, 37–38, 45–47, 157–58
Snow-birds, 117–18
Snow plant, 75, 111
Soda Springs, 11, 154, 155, 157, 158, 163, 164
South Dome, 54; climbing, 123–24; glaciers and, 127; summit, 126; view from, 125–26, 126–27
Sparrows, 118, 121
Spiraea, 126, 191
Spruce. *See* Douglas spruce
Stanislaus grove, 107
Starr King Cone, 127, 141
Starr King Dome, 139, 142, 147; glaciers and, 127; red cedar on, 88; primrose at, 110
Stellar's jays, 117, 121–22, 127
Streams, 31–32, 49–51

Taluses, origin of, 56–64; trees on, 79
Tamarack Creek Fall, 24
Tenaya, Chief, 8, 168–74
Tenaya basin, 138; glaciers and, 134; lakes in, 12
Tenaya Canon, 9–10, 26; glaciers and, 134; naming of, 174

Index

WOMEN IN CHURCH HISTORY